Southern Lights

Southern Lights

**PEN American Center/South's
Annual Literary Review**

Southern Lights
Literary Review
PEN American Center/South
(Formerly PEN Gulf South)

Editor: *Skye Kathleen Moody*
Guest Editor and Contributor: *Louise McKinney*
Editorial and Layout Consultant: *Barbara Porter*
Art Direction: *MF Designs*

Published once a year. **Manya DeLeon Booksmith,** New Orleans, LA. For copies, send a check for $10 to:

Southern Lights
c/o PEN American Center/South
501 rue Burgundy
New Orleans, Louisiana 70112, USA
504-522-8985

No part of this book may be reproduced or transmitted in any form or by any means electronic or mechanical, including photocopying, recording, or by any information storage or retrieval system without prior written permission from the publisher or the individual authors.

Individual copyrights remain with the authors.

© 1995

All rights reserved.

First printing 1995.

ISBN 0-9638061-1-4

Dolphin Press, Inc., Long Beach, MS 39560

Cover design by Melanie Ferniz
Cover photo illustration by Skye Kathleen Moody

Southern Lights
PEN American Center/South's Annual Literary Review

Manya DeLeon Booksmith
940 Royal Street, Suite 201
New Orleans, LA 70116
USA

Acknowledgment

The editors of *Southern Lights* wish to gratefully acknowledge invaluable contributions by Manya L. DeLeon, Barbara Porter, Peter Phillips of Dolphin Press and Melanie Ferniz of MF Designs.

Table of Contents

	Page
Acknowledgment	vi
Preface	ix
Introduction: Sense/less of Place	
Steven G. Kellman............................	1
Pulling Away	
June Akers Seese...............................	5
Poems	
Robert Phillips.................................	15
Son of Obituaries	
Richard Grayson..............................	18
Poems	
Lisa Kahn..	22
Four Knights Opening	
Sergei Task	
Translated from the Russian by	
Marian Schwartz...............................	36
Faux Pas: Origins of the Social Blunder in Human Civilization	
Skye Kathleen Moody........................	53
Four *Faux Pas* and Why to Avoid Them	
Margin of Hydra...............................	60

A Cellblock Mass
    Raymond Schroth, S.J. 72
Poems
    Louise McKinney 83
The Films of Theo Angelopoulos:
Beyond the Borders
    Andrew Horton 97
Journal: Saturday, October 20th
    Richard Grayson 104
Biographies   108
About PEN   115

Preface

When William Faulkner wrote *Soldiers' Pay* in a New Orleans townhouse in Pirate's Alley overlooking St. Louis Cathedral's gardens, he never suspected that, decades later, his Muse would haunt the South, striking writer after writer with her inspirational lightning rod.

The Southern United States hangs heavy with Muses. They fall from a sultry sky like ponderous lavender wisteria, vines clutching our senses; their inspirational songs, perfume and poison, set our creative genes to swooning.

Muses ride the Southwestern desert, diligent as Texas Rangers chasing us. From armadilloland into the *cha-cha marimba* rhythms over San Antonio, the South's Muses swell and strain like Debussy sirens, striking the unwary writer whose words ache for mustang power.

Thrashing through Louisiana swamps, fiercer than summer locusts, slicker than a nutria's coat, they prowl us. When we least suspect, they hit with a force even hurricane shutters can't keep out. Wordspill bloodies our mind's page; poems and novels are conceived, gestated and some, nurtured to life. Fickle, passionate partners, our Muses won't be ignored.

Southern Muses flow up across an Ozark's spine; chilling and raw-boned, they drive down upon Georgia's Blue Ridge Mountains, then amble blithely into pulsing Atlanta. Through Georgia, Alabama and Mississippi, they kick up blood red rusted soil and, out of this and hot, soft summer rains, fashion the most eccentric and poignant storytellers: Eudora Welty, Carson McCullers, Flannery

O'Conner and newer voices like June Akers Seese and Robert Phillips, Lisa Kahn, Ernest Gaines and Robert Olen Butler.

In Key West, Hemingway's Muse rocks a restless novelist's boat until it capsizes. Along the Gulf Coast, Faulkner's spirit shouts at the horizon and the Muse echoes back into piney woods where Walker Evans' inspiration haunts naysayers of compassionate literature. They never rest, these Southern Muses, but constantly spin their word tornadoes, chasing a Floridian essayist down long white deserted beaches, and in New Orleans, resurrecting Neo-Gothic vampires and worshipping dunces.

In a cowboy's boot, on the alligator's snout, in the velvet glove and Panama hat, the New South harbors more exotic mystery and drama than a Carnival torchlight parade before a Quadroon ball. And herein lies a key to a Southern Muse's vitality: who isn't, after all, a Quadroon at a masked ball? Such rich complex mystery blesses and plagues a region where often the air hangs too heavy to think straight, so you just write what's landed on your soul and pray it makes sense.

Welcome to America's PEN South Literary Review. *Southern Lights* is a vehicle expressing a rich everflowing vein of PEN talent. This volume's Guest Editor and Contributing Writer, Canadian Louise McKinney, has been a Friend of PEN International for many years.

This premier issue is dedicated to the Muse in all of us.

Skye Kathleen Moody

April, 1995
New Orleans, Louisiana

Southern Lights

Introduction

Sense/less of Place

Steven G. Kellman

"There's a place for us," sing Tony and Maria, but wherever that place might be it is surely not on the West Side of Manhattan. In a violent, crowded urban landscape that leaves no place for romance, their youthful yearning to be elsewhere is utopian, in the sense Thomas More drew upon when he minted the term from Greek roots for *no place*. There is, according to the venerable song, no place like home, but Thomas Wolfe's mobile homeland is the place where you can't go home, again or ever.

North America has not only served as a site for utopian experiments—Brook Farm, New Harmony, and numerous other communes and sodalities—but the continent's vast, ambiguous land mass has itself seemed utopia to many who, like Kafka in *Amerika*, could imagine a Pacific Coast in Oklahoma. "It avails not, time nor place—distance avails not," proclaims Whitman in a denial of geography that he shares with many of his compatriots. "In the United States there is more space where nobody is than where anybody is," wrote Gertrude Stein in *The*

Geographical History of America. "That is what makes America what it is." When Huck Finn lights out for the territory ahead, the tracts have not been platted. "I am not a Virginian, but an American," announced Patrick Henry to the First Continental Congress, in 1774. Raising—and pulling up—the stakes, William Lloyd Garrison declared: "My country is the world; my countrymen are mankind."

And yet local fiefdoms dot the map of American literature. Faulkner in Yoknapatawpha, Steinbeck in Salinas, Bellow in Chicago, Cather in Nebraska, Hemingway in Upper Michigan, Olson in Gloucester, Glasgow in Virginia, Wharton in New York, Thoreau at Walden Pond, Chopin in Louisiana, Chandler in Los Angeles, Jewett in the country of the pointed firs—each author holds imaginary deed to a particular plot. It is as ludicrous to envision Flannery O'Connor poaching on William Kennedy's Albany as it is to issue one of Joyce's Dubliners a visa to Hardy's Wessex or García Marquez's Macondo. For all its utopian impulses, its global and even cosmic ambitions, much American literature is a proprietary chronicle of neighborhood news.

Emily Dickinson, the most localized of major authors, created her "letter to the world" by withdrawing from it, by spending most of her fifty-six years secluded in an Amherst household. Yet her vocabulary, rich in references to Death, Faith, Love, and Immortality, is purged of the distinctive dialect of immediate environs. The poetry offers scant evidence for positioning its author in western Massachusetts rather than Winesburg, Ohio; Paumanok, New York; Cross Creek, Florida; Gopher Prairie, Minnesota; Spoon River, Illinois; Paterson, New Jersey; Thalia, Texas; Asheville, North Carolina; or Hannibal, Missouri. "To generalize is to be an idiot," generalized William Blake. "To particularize is the alone distinction of merit. General knowledges are those knowledges that idiots possess." Dickinson was no idiot, though she managed to avoid the postmarks of space and time that stamp so many other American writers. Confined to one terse zone, she made the globe her home, entering the abstract without first stepping on concrete.

A sense of place would seem to have little place in a republic of letters whose citizens are poets, playwrights, essayists, editors, and novelists from all over the world. It was a utopian—i.e., idealistic—dream of effacing national boundaries and tribal rivalries that led to PEN. The global association was founded in 1921 as a literary antidote to the lethal factionalism that threw authors and others into trenches and coffins just a few years before. The existence of an international writers' organization did not avert another World War or the participation of writers as polemicists, combatants, and victims. Hitler, Mussolini, and Churchill were all very successful writers. Of all the arts, except perhaps architecture, literature remains most closely yoked to place. While language is enlisted to draft a Universal Declaration of Human Rights, it is also, and more easily, the unfungible currency of a sovereign province. While paintings, sonatas, and films can travel more or less on their own, books demand translation. Their medium—words—is local. No one ever wrote the Great American Novel or the Great Malayan Pantoum in Esperanto. Writers, like chefs, assemble and confect their concoctions out of regional produce. They write in the shadow of Babel.

So PEN is organized into national centers that sometimes, as in the spat over whether to hold an international congress in Croatia in 1993, allow allegiance to a flag to supersede devotion to the Muse. The PEN Charter, a declaration of aesthetic universalism, demands that: "In all circumstances, and particularly in time of war, the patrimony of humanity at large should be left untouched by national or political passion." So, too, have labor leaders fancied that workers of the world would unite even in times of conflict between states. Some governments have, defying PEN's commitment to the fundamental freedom to write, attempted to control PEN chapters, to manipulate them as instruments of official policy. Tyrants try to keep writers in their place, as if writing were a function of place, and place were a position to be established by the state.

Some nations, like multilingual Canada and Switzerland, have mutated into geometrical oddities with more than one PEN center. English is spoken at both PEN American Center, based in New York, and PEN USA West, based in Los Angeles, and each extends its franchise into overlapping regional chapters. The "Gulf South" Chapter of PEN American Center covers seven states—Alabama, Arkansas, Florida, Georgia, Louisiana, Mississippi, and Texas—whose members surely feel a different sense of place than those in the Midwest, New England, Northwest, and West chapters. But the region defined by "Gulf South" sprawls so far that it is more than a single place. Two of the seven states in "Gulf South," Arkansas and Georgia, do not even abut the Gulf of Mexico. Alabama barely does. Georgia probably has more in common with South Carolina, which is not in the chapter, than it does with Texas, which itself encompasses two time zones and at least five distinct dialects and shares borders and terrain with Oklahoma and New Mexico.

But if distance avails not, a poet in Hattiesburg can be neighbor to a playwright in Ghana. To the literary imagination, Athens, Georgia, and Athens, Greece, Oxford, Mississippi, and Oxford, England, are contiguous. And if Dickinson had been able to transmit a letter to the world by e-mail, the cartographical coordinates of Amherst might have seemed even less significant. To an avid writer, or reader, place means nothing and everything.

Pulling Away

June Akers Seese

Note: *These chapters are excerpted from a novel-in-progress titled,* A Nurse Can Go Anywhere.

Preface
    The first time I did "it" was on a Sunday afternoon. Baptists were forbidden to go to the movies on Sunday. Likewise to play cards, dance, or miss services in the evening. So after Sunday School, after the noon meal, in the attic while the whole family slept, I discovered how quick and quiet it could be.

Pulling Away
    I was a foundling. The family who took me in could never be mistaken for my parents. I was short and thin and covered with freckles. They were giants. My mother was so tall, special cupboards were built for her so she wouldn't have to stoop during canning season. They weren't mean people, but a farm is not just a husband and wife. I had an uncle, my mother's brother, who lived on the place. He behaved himself when my father was around. Not a hired hand, though we had them too.
    "Where's the bastard?" my uncle would say, always knowing where I was. The last time he said it I was fourteen. Alone in the house. Quail season was over, the windows were open, and he was walking toward me. I picked up the shotgun my father had left on the sideboard and aimed at his stomach. He walked backwards toward

the kitchen door. I can't remember calling my father, but I did and he came with the police. My uncle was drunk. He hadn't always been drunk, but he'd called me that name from the beginning. Bastard. You don't hear it used for its rightful purpose now. Even illegitimate doesn't apply anymore. Then it applied. We lived by the good book. Sundays we labored all day for Jesus. "No rest for the wicked," my uncle said, looking at me over the lumpy potatoes. I had been baptized and pushed and prayed over by then, and I knew what was expected of me.

The first time I got laid was on Sunday afternoon. They say suffering is redemptive, but it was not a religious experience. The second time was not much better. A willow tree didn't help, and I don't remember the day of that week. I must be doing something wrong, I thought, blaming myself as usual. My uncle was dead by then, and I was a nurse. In those days, nurses always wore white and a special hat to separate good training from bad.

The week before Christmas, the year he died, I was working in the O.R. when the police brought in a man on a stretcher. As soon as I realized it was my uncle, I pulled away.

The doctor said, "We're all going in on this one."

"Not me," I said. "He's ruined every Christmas we ever had, and I'm not going to see to it he ruins this one."

Of course I came to my senses, and we brought him around. He lay in intensive care until New Year's. My mother came early every day, but my father ate dinner with me in the cafeteria before he, too, took the elevator up. His favorite hymn, *When the Roll Is Called Up Yonder*, he hummed as we picked our way through the canned peas. "A bright and cloudless morning," I thought. "When time shall be no more," I continued, wondering about my future.

The funeral came and went. It rained that winter. Bleak days that appeared hopeless. The ground looked like tobacco would never grow again. But I felt free and happy.
Once you kiss the church and your family goodbye, there's not much left in a Carolina town; but a nurse can go anywhere. I went straight to hell.

Beatings
Everybody beat their kids in those days, and beatings were better than getting your fingers bent back or having to hang the yellowed bed sheets on the screened porch banister before you left the house in the morning. My father used a razor strap, and I can still smell the leather. I know I cried. I remember I never got more than three licks, and missing supper was a relief because I didn't feel like eating anyway. What I can't remember is why I got the beatings. They came in the evening long after I had made my mistake, and they ended when I was six years old. School must have had a good influence on me. My mother said it did. The beatings were easier than listening to my uncle's homilies. I guess my father had given up on Bible verses years back, though he would never admit it. He liked hymns, but he was good at forgetting his early training. I guess I got my poor memory from him.

Where Can I Go Now?
I used the back of my spelling tablet for lists. I liked to count. By age ten, I was keeping track of how many redheads were in my school and which yards had a willow tree. Before I settled on nursing, I spent a lot of time thinking about home ec. Chemistry was my best class. I could have taught school. I'm a good cook, too. All the mixing and precision. You can see what a hard choice it was. And in the end, money mattered the most. Nurses were paid in time and stayed in the hospital; the

uniforms kept you equal and there was a real paycheck at the end of each rotation. Of course, I hoped to go back for the degree, and may still, but for what happened to me, the flash of light, the E.R., and the doctors: one after the other, neurologist after neurologist. "Faulty wiring," they said. Me or the hospital where it happened?

Now I'm working some on the weekends—private duty here in Atlanta. Once I made the decision, I saw it was the right one.

But back to the days when I thought recipes mattered and I brought chemistry beakers back to my bedroom to hold the single stem I kept on my bedside stand.

Where is anywhere? Where can any woman go?

I was wrong about nursing. After the accident, everything changed.

Nurses are trained to expect and deal with vomit, shit and pee and to call them all by formal names. Nurses are expected to confront the outer reality, be it bloody or broken. They are expected to act and record their actions. They are expected to follow orders. Patients die. The orders are not always correct. But the suffering continues. Nurses must watch it and record what they see. In nursing, time seems to count. And measurements.

Listening to Louella Explain the Curse

Every farm community has its leader, and ours was a product of the untended life we lived. Louella took us to a filthy swamp—frozen over in winter and full of bends and enclosures where skating was endured for privacy. We stumbled behind her. Our cheeks were flushed. Tall reeds stopped any skater bent on uninterrupted swirls and flourishes. We were members of Louella's sex club with its meeting place under a tree stump her brother had hollowed out to hide his thin pale balloons. She would explain all that later; now we need

only bring her dimes to learn the facts our parents hid from us.
 She told us about periods. We could have one if we let her put her finger far up inside our bodies where she would pop our cherries.
 "Would it hurt?" we cowered. "It would be worth it," she stoutly evaded our fears.
 She also had a bullet-shaped water pistol that she offered the oldest of us, if we would first push it in and out of her—faster, slosh-sloshing and watching her face sweat and a grimace twist her lips. We learned more about power than sex. Our discovering of these forbidden practices, the lies to be unlearned later. . .our excitement was boundless.

Cream of Wheat

 My first taste of freedom came on Saturday. The bus passed our farm at 9:30 and returned before suppertime. My mother suggested a movie, lunch at the drugstore, and shopping; yet the money she sent along did not cover all three.
 A carefully dressed woman with no neck rode the bus every Saturday. She had a good figure, but she couldn't bend her head. White gloves, and a neatly folded shopping bag from the week before, sat on her lap. Another regular was a taciturn man who had once been handsome, but now was a drunk on his way to town on some pretext, sure to come back in the afternoon with a red face and unsnapped boots, without a hat, his reprocessed wool jacket unbuttoned, garrulous with the new driver. He always sat in the vertical seats near the driver's head.
 I was content to watch the no-necked woman. She had a humped back, too, though her heavy Chesterfield disguised it. Five miles passed before we stopped for another passenger.

The two booths at the drugstore waited at the end of the soda fountain, not sought after until 11:00 a.m. when I slid onto the torn plastic to consider my choices. All the sandwiches came with potato chips and thin pickle slices. Their stuffings were mixed with mayonnaise and sweet relish, their freshness doubtful. My mother never passed a lunch counter without reminding me of the connection between warm mayonnaise and food poisoning. She said these sandwich fillings were mixed ahead, sometimes days ahead, and were ripe for a rise in temperature that would make them agents of destruction. True, it was winter, but I felt the delicious possibility of danger as I tasted spicy ham salad mashed against a triangle of Wonder Bread.

Buses stopped outside the window of my booth. The lines were long, and snow fell steadily. Gray, sloppy galoshes, faded wool coats and babushkas protected the women who had to take this bus to go grocery shopping. Never thinking their fate might one day be mine, I felt rich with change in my pocket and an afternoon of surprises waiting.

The movie opened its doors at noon, so there was time to buy popcorn and walk up the slope bordered by gilt rectangles framing the coming attractions. Inside, the huge screen with its Pathon news, cartoons, travel shorts, collections for the soldiers in Germany and polio here at home, and more previews made the double feature which followed a true all-day sucker. I did not go to the kiddie movies across town because the mess, the noise, and the camaraderie frightened me. I had no use for Walt Disney.

I found a companion for these excursions when I was thirteen. Shirley didn't like movies, but she loved shopping—shoplifting as it became—and we stole the smallest, most useless trifles the dime store offered. Then we ate Friday's leftovers at her brother's apartment eight blocks away. Before we could begin dating together (she was boy-crazy, my mother said), my mother forbade me to leave the house on Saturday. Shirley wore pancake makeup, short skirts, and skin-tight sweaters. Her brown hair was thin. No pins or rubber bands could help it. It was not hard to picture her with a baby in a few years, standing with the other women in front of the drug store's plate glass window. As for me, I waited by the radio wondering when I would be too old for *Let's Pretend:* "Cream of Wheat is so good to eat that we have it every day; we sing this song, it will make us strong and it makes us shout hooray!"

Saving Dreams
Remember the dreams of your childhood? I can remember the kaleidoscope of colors behind my eyelids when I pressed my fingers on them—crazy patterns in primary colors that changed and moved until the blackness behind my closed eyelids returned. These reds and blues and yellows shaped by unknown things reappeared in my dreams. This I remember, but I have lost the nightmare.

Its content is gone; no efforts to remember work.

I sit at this kitchen table on Friday until late night television ends, hoping the everydayness of gunfire and canned laughter will help me remember. Something important is missing. Something that will make sense of my life, and make all the time I sit alone lead to something. That one nightmare is the key. Patiently, I hold this sentence in my mind. Earnestly I wait.

I dream every night, and I try to write the dreams in a notebook, but the faded shadow of Nicole Brown floats against the scales of justice; and that awful music distracts me. I try to concentrate on the voice of Marcia Clark: ". . .he took her youth, her freedom, and her self-respect; then Orenthal James Simpson took her very life. . ." Why do these words cut me? My uncle is dead—buried under one of those ugly granite slabs; and I have left the whole town long behind me. I have never gone back. Eventually

I am able to focus; and I watch the witnesses and the lawyers. I listen hard. The music begins at noon and ends at three. I stare at the wall until 4:30 when the shadow of Nicole again crosses the television screen. I don't answer the phone until the sun goes down.

Unspoken Thoughts

A nurse can go anywhere, and here I am weighted down in travel brochures. "Anywhere," I think to myself, waiting at the bus stop, hoping the man next to me with the walking stick will have something to say. Sun means more than it ever did, and there is no sun today.

Only the trucks pass. The owner of *Small Carpenters At Large* waves. He remodeled my apartment. He told me the truth about dogs: "Don't bother," he said. "Barking won't help," he continued. It's some comfort to know he lives eight doors away. It's some comfort to know Atlanta is a city.

Nightmare

Dreams throw fear to the surface. Last night I was pursued by hired killers who rode with rifles on a big semi and sought me out wherever I ran: to a big, empty hotel where all the closets and rooms were unlockable, to the dirt yard of a family of eight where I begged the father to shoot my pursuers and hide me. Crawling and breathless, I lay at his feet, while the all-seeing gunmen leaped from the truck, pulled the trigger and water turned the clay yard to mud.

The killer had a face just like the face of a man who hangs around the old school at the end of the block. He paces up and down the intersection. When it rains, he sits on a bench with a faded insurance company ad on its wood. His tennis shoes have laces meant for basketball high-tops, so he is always tripping on them. He has a smoothly shaven face and a trim haircut, but his coat is full of holes and his shirt collars need to be turned. He looks at his feet as he walks, at his hands when he sits. Once I saw him in the alley leaning against the newly painted Dempsey Dumpster. A maggot rested near his shoulder, and his feet were surrounded by blackened lettuce leaves. The law is too busy betting the horses to give a damn what goes on in the alley or the street. Besides, he can't do anything about a man waiting quietly.

Toilet Training
Why would anyone want to run away from home to a "comfort station"? I did. Was it the title of the little house set off and separated from the sidewalk by a lawn and curved walk? Was it the price? "Our taxes pay for it," my mother said. Time spent in the stalls and at the sinks was free, though nobody imagined a person would want to stay all night. Was it privacy? Only cleaning ladies and other girls and women came there—intermittently, too. Or was the reason complicated? Does it relate to soiling and Freud and the unconscious? I don't know. I do know that that house was the protagonist in my dreams for years. It held its own place in my daytime fantasies, too.

I wondered if they checked to see who was in the stalls, if the cleaning ladies changed daily? I knew I would be found eventually, but I wondered how long I could have the warmth and independence the building offered. It was the only place I saw that hinted at the promise of free shelter for the night. Park benches, the seats at the bus station, and the library sofas were cleared at regular intervals by policemen, but I had never seen the law in these toilets.

I welcomed these germs my mother had warned against. Public toilets, home of strange and terrible diseases found on uncovered toilet seats. I would sleep here with my legs propped against the door. No one would see me. And in the morning, I could leave. Money would be no problem; I had a bank full of quarters and a drawer with 23 crisp dollar bills waiting in a brown envelope.

I was ready. Sleeping in my underwear. Waiting for the day when I was strong enough to go hide before the 8:00 bus pulled out of the dirt turnaround. What sort of punishment would I get? I imagined something worse than a whipping, but what that might be did not enter my head. So the fear of that unknown day of reckoning destroyed my bravery and kept me in a state of imagining where I planned, with small variations, over and over, a trip I dared not take. The nearest I came was locking my own bathroom door and pushing my face against the cold tub with my legs pressed together and my heart pounding. I was fourteen years old when I realized the name for the feeling of relief between my legs.

Robert Phillips

The Ruined Man

To be a ruined man can be a vocation.
                            — **T. S. Eliot**
                          on S. T. Coleridge

He had a vision, trained for it like an Olympian,
with absolute dedication, year out and year in.

At college he lost his scholarship in Engineering.
He managed that in one fall term and one spring.

His next feat was to take a wife and father a son,
then lose them both. This loss was hard-won.

When he spoke, his voice emerged a thin mumble.
He lived in one rented room, his clothes a jungle.

He never put sheets on the bed, avoided the fuss.
He ate out of cans, not once put up a Christmas

tree. Visiting his small son, he gifted him
with a stick of gum. His car had no chrome trim.

He applied for a little job in a big corporate
headquarters. On a slide rule he slid estimates

in the same cubicle for forty years. After eight
P.M. he haunted the Greyhound depot, calculating

why transients and travelers enter and egress,
strangers from Schenectady, Buffalo, Lake Success.

It was entertainment. He had nowhere else to go.
Winters that city accumulated 120 inches of snow.

Inconspicuously hunched on a slat bench there,
he blew unfiltered Camel rings into the air.

("He's just being a good Christian," his droll
schizophrenic son surmised. "It's in the Bible:

'It is easier for a Camel to go between
the Needle's Eye than a rich man to enter Heaven.' ")

It took sixty-plus years to get it all undone;
eventually he destroyed throat, esophagus, lungs.

When they claimed him to undergo the knife,
he took solace in the perfection of his life.

Sixth Decade Haiku

   i.

The box they gave him
  on retirement held a watch
that measures decades.

   ii.

His dead wife's false teeth
  underfoot in their bedroom.
Feel the piercing chill!

   iii.

The new bifocals
  rest in their satin-lined case,
his body coffined.

Son of Obituaries

Richard Grayson

Mrs. Sanjour, our ninth grade English teacher at J.H.S. 253 back in Brooklyn, told us that reading the *New York Times* every day was what separated civilized humans from barbarians. I think of Mrs. Sanjour sometimes when I pick up the blue plastic containing the national edition of the *Times* on my doorstep at 6:30 a.m. It's been years since I lived in New York, but I've been compulsively reading the *Times* ever since I've been on my own. In college I lived at home and would usually buy it only when they had a big banner eight-column (now they have six wider-columns) headline announcing some momentous or catastrophic event ("MEN WALK ON MOON") or when there was some political news I was particularly interested in.

Back in junior high, we could subscribe to the *Herald Tribune* and get copies in homeroom, but Mrs. Sanjour sniffed that it was a pale imitation of the *Times*. (Actually, the *Herald Tribune* was pretty lively in the mid-60s, although the paper soon merged with two others and then died.) As long as she was trying to wean us off the tabloids our parents brought home (my grandfather read the *Daily News*, "New York's picture newspaper," and every evening my father brought home the *Post,* in its pre-sensationalist days when I thought of it as the liberal-Jewish paper), she might as well introduce us to the real thing.

Mrs. Sanjour made us get the *Sunday Times* every week and she tested us on it on Mondays. She showed us how to find the hidden Ninas in the Hirschfield cartoons of Broadway stars that were on the front page of Section 2 every Sunday. She never asked questions about Section 3, business (which she didn't understand) or Section 5, sports (knowing that was what most boys would read anyway—even if you could hardly tell who won the game in the dense thickets of the prose). Instead she concentrated on Section 2, arts and leisure; Section 4, the news of the week in review (with its page of editorial cartoons culled from other newspapers; the *Times* not only did not have comics, they were so serious they didn't have their own editorial cartoonist); the magazine and the book review, although Mrs. Sanjour admitted the latter two would often print articles "above a ninth-grader's head"; and of course the first section of news.

The questions on her quizzes would be on the order of: Who was Arturo Frondizi? (President of Argentina—you couldn't have missed that big glossy magazine that the Argentine government had put in the paper as a 96-page advertisement.) Who was Art Carney's co-star? (Walter Matthau, in *The Odd Couple*—this years before the movie or TV show, when kids our age had never heard of Felix and Oscar.)

One Monday Mrs. Sanjour was absent, and through the grapevine we ninth graders learned that her husband had died suddenly the day before. Mrs. Newman, our homeroom and Spanish teacher—who had been Baby Peggy in the movies, but that's another story—was Mrs. Sanjour's best friend. She tearfully told the class that Mrs. Sanjour's husband had died of a heart attack. "I bet it was after he tried to lift yesterday's paper," the kid next to me whispered. The substitute English teacher didn't give us a quiz; she probably didn't even read the *Times* herself.

Now that I get the national edition, in my obsessive-compulsive way, I read it bizarrely. I scan the headlines on the front page and then I separate the three sections. The first, the hard news and editorial and op-ed, is usually 12, 14, or 16 pages. I open the section to the middle page and then tear the paper in two. Then I pair up two pages. If I can find two pages with ads, I put them in the middle of the pair so I can just read one outside page and then the other. Otherwise I read the outside pages of each pair and then read the inside pages. I do the same thing with the arts and living section, discarding sports (I was not one of those boys who would have read the sports pages on my own). With the business section, I throw out at least half the pages because they feature the stock tables and I've owned only one stock since I was in junior high: ten shares of Martin Marietta which my grandfather gave me for my bar mitzvah. I pair up the other pages and read them back to back.

Since about 1984, I've been scanning the obituaries page differently. I not only read the printed obituaries of "Executive who led a commuter airline" or "Magician who aided the police" or "Civic leader in West," but I scan the death notices, the ones people pay for. It's the smallest print in the paper, the print they use for classified ads, but actually small print is getting easier for me to read these days as my eyes adjust to middle age. There's a listing of each person who's got at least one death notice. Obviously the computer system that scans the names has some bugs in it because it doesn't catch variations in first names, so you'll have "Bernstein, Sid," listed above "Bernstein, Sidney," and if someone's death notice is for "Smith, H. Parker," it'll come out on the list as "Smith, H." People in religious orders often have their first name listed as "Brother" or "Sister" or "Monsignor."

Sometimes in reading the lists of people—about once every two weeks—I'll see the name of someone I know: the widow of the psychiatrist I saw as a teenager; my father's second cousin; often a professor I had at Brooklyn College. But what I'm really looking for are young men's names—or what I think are young men's names: Todd, Andrew, Marc, Evan, Brad, Jay, Scott, Jermaine. Some names, like David, might be young men but they also can be 97-year-old great-grandfathers who gave up the ghost in Miami Beach. I check any name I think might belong to someone who died of AIDS and then I read their death notice to find out. There are usually one or two. Sometimes I think the number of people who died of AIDS (whether it says it straight out or not, you can tell) is going down, but then some days there seem to be five or six young men, 32 or 46 or 39, fashion designers or attorneys or just men with companions or surviving parents and grandparents, and I realize that the epidemic is still going as strong as ever.

Today there's a "Cohen, Michael," which could be a two-year-old or an octogenarian until I read the death notice:

"COHEN—Michael. June 17, 1954 to August 3, 1993. Died after a lousy rotten illness. Friends remember his irascible quest. A true believer, he always knew there was No Place Like Home. Donations to GMHC or God's Love We Deliver."

Is this the Michael Cohen I remember from College? Stephen LiMandri's friend? Stephen never referred to him as Michael but always as "Michael Cohen," probably to distinguish him from all the other Michaels we knew. I'm not even sure I ever was introduced to him; maybe I just saw him around. I remember Stephen met him in Macy's at the perfume counter when they were both buying presents for Mother's Day. I think he was blond and wore glasses, but that may only be because Stephen told me that. Michael Cohen is a very common name.

Lisa Kahn

Inexorable Puzzles

I.

perhaps
she does not know
could it be
that they do not know each
other anymore?

Sitting alone on her sunset bench
in front of the cabin from hand-felled
oaken logs that memories encroach
amalgamate dissolve solidify again
then soften

how many times has she sat here
with the young boy the teenager
the student savoring his country breakfasts
—eggs over easy—
the strong coffee freshly brewed
his eager shouting "MOOOOther get up
breakfast's ready!"
a call for which she had been waiting
in joyful anticipation since the
start of the clanging and banging
of pans and kitchen utensils

while the sweet scales of the
Rhenish by Mendelssohn dropped
—liquid silver—into her ears
it was her favorite record in
those years next to Bloch's
Voices in the Wilderness for
which he did not care so much
calling it "too somber" so it
was for her sake when he put it
on at all

tender emotions would creep into
her throat then she would kiss
his ear his hair and he would suffer
it silently would not withdraw
they would look content at the
grazing Herefords as with bent
heads they chewed and chewed
they would glance at the waves
of verdant grass and corn
rippling in gentle breezes
would discuss their dreams and
aspirations the wonders of the
chambered nautilus which he tried
to trace under electromicroscopes
the lyrics they would compose
together which would be titled
"Divertimentos"

they laughed a lot and yet and yet
these were not carefree times
were full of haunting memories and
nightmares *sans merci* though they
would rarely admit it to each other

II.

During these years of sorrows past
and present and of laughter
did she know
really *know*
this boy with lanky arms and legs
forced by fate to grow into manhood
all too fast? This son who wanted
to protect her while she tried hard
to spare him further blows and
losses? This boy who always had
to prove himself competing with
his own best friends outshining
his own best efforts counting
his honors and successes as if
survival would depend on everyone's
approval? Did she who loved him
so unconditionally fail to convince
him of her affection admiration
love?

On one occasion she could no longer
contain her bewilderment and blurted
out how she loved him absolutely
how he did not have to *earn* her
love! That were he less gifted
less intelligent less diligent less
everything she'd love him just the
same! He seemed surprised he nodded
silently

once she insulted him or so it seemed
expressing thoughts too blunt for
him: "if you were sick or handicapped

or retarded you think I'd love you
less?" she yelled watching how his
face turned stony he went for a walk
and when at long last he returned
they avoided the topic
she could feel or seemed to feel
resentment emanating from the way
he lifted his shoulder blades and
later his left brow
so she remained on guard and careful
always to give him full verbal
measure of her praise for his
admirable exemplary ambitious
strivings

III.

Perhaps she does not know
not really
she got to know him better when
he left home? There were few letters
and—as mothers will—she tried
to read between the lines
surely there were occasional
phone calls but he had a gift
for writing it seemed a shame
to let this talent go to waste

he worked hard now proving to the
world his knowledge and his
motivation it would have been
futile for her to ask other than
superficial questions the probing
might have diminished his
affection which she craved so

she responded with congratulations
expressions of pride and joy
they were sincere and he deserved
them

she had wondered when he left
home in which direction his
inclinations would lead him
during infrequent visits she
could sense that he had turned
more critical towards friends
towards colleagues and towards her:
"Mother you *must!*" "How *can* you!"
"How can you *not!*"

when sitting now alone on the sunset
bench her heart would run to him
leap over fields stumble through
thickets climb peaks hurl itself
recklessly into evil-smelling carnivorous
bowels of monster-cities swim across
oceans shout like Abraham: "Here I am!
Here I am!" Did he ever hear her?

IV.

Then his wedding in the verdant
country-side of May indelibly in-
scribed in her memory: carpets of
wild-flowers abloom solemn promises
merry-making in the log cabin
lowing of cattle and the Spanish moss
beards of patriarchal life-oaks
swinging gently in the breeze
whispering secrets and his wife whom
she had known for many years

kindling hope that he might gradually
change his priorities turn less harsh

now the threesome would sometimes
sit on the bench for breakfast
chattering pleasantly watching the
silent Herefords chew and chew and
in the background of their conversations
the Mendelssohn again but not the Bloch
for his mood was "upbeat" as he
called it so the Grieg and Schumann
piano concertos were added or flamencos
played by Manitas de Plata

but these were also the years when he
stopped painting sketching sculpting
composing working on his novel
writing poetry for such superfluous
leisure pursuits were too time-
consuming now that his concerns
centered around the farm which she
—he claimed—had so neglected
she felt hurt for she had given her
full attention to it so she believed
and as much time and care as a slowly
aging widow whose energies were spent
yet not replenished possibly could

did he not know how the banal burdens
of everyday demands encroached on her?
But he was young and eager full of plans:
bulldozers invaded the privacy of
pastures erazed the soil's hair dug
holes for ponds into the earth's flesh
new cattle white and yellowish and ugly

was bought because these Simmentals
grow faster thus promising more profit!
He mended fences installed more cattle-
guards shredded sprayed planted till
his body collapsed at night was he
afraid of dreams? Old dreams? New
dreams? Nightmares? What had happened
to his many artistic inclinations?
His aesthetic pleasures?

His wife whom she had known for many
years defended him insisted: "He needs
the workout it is good for him he sits
all week long in his office he should
exercise his body here!"
Did his wife
perhaps
know him better?
This strange man who as the years
passed by seemed to turn stranger
still? Or had she simply projected
her own goals onto him? Wanted to
live vicariously through him? Had
assumed he would paint and sing and
write forever? Because she had
desired it so?

V.

Perhaps
she does not know
or knows no longer
his aims and goals and purpose
for when his small son inquisitive
and angel-faced would join them on
the sunset bench for breakfast it

seemed as if his father was too
strict and too demanding expecting
the little one to perform beyond
his years

one day she gathered the small remaining
coins of courage left her and asked
softly almost timidly: "Why this
particular road? Why?" He answered
brusquely: "Because I will not suffer
fools gladly: Will not let others
step on my toes: Not let them do me in
like they did father! You should have
noticed the direction years ago!
Did you suppose I could forget the
past? Ever forget it?" His generous
full mouth turned into a pencil-line
his knuckles clenched his eyes
avoided hers
she bent her head
was this the legacy his father left him?
When he left him?

VI.

Today is Lag Ba 'Omer
the mystic festival in May of which
he does not know being agnostic and
a bit too proud of it
sitting again alone on the sunset
bench she reflects and fears and
hopes surely she had never expected
him to forget! How could he! How could
she! Yet she had so fervently wished
that he had made peace with their past
the tendrils of memories keep

growing: Breakfast with the *Rhenish*
the long relinquished eggs over easy
poetry and painting laughing
now she gazes at the Herefords
and the Simmentals silently chewing
and chewing as she chews her sorrow
her sadness puts a tape of the Bloch
on again which had been abandoned
long ago

the directions he takes cannot be
willed by her whose life is spent
well spent and ill spent like most
lives are her loneliness seems an
appropriate preparation for facing
death who will be friend and brother

then she listens to the *Prelude* and
Fugue In C-Major by Bach which makes
the faintness of heart subside and
uplifted by the rippling scales
and strands variations and harmonies
her ardent wishes for him blossom

The Piles of Shoes
Holocaust Museum, Washington, D.C.

The piles and piles of
ashen-colored canvas shoes

piles on the left
piles on the right
large shoes and little shoes
women's men's and children's
they cry out: *Where*
are the feet which walked
in us? What did you do with
them? What did you permit the
murderers to do with them?

one pair—which one?—
must have carried your feet
Beatrice
did they falter?
Did they trip?
Did they tremble
on their way in the camp
of Osciwice which we call
Auschwitz?

Did these feet—ice cold
long before life left them—

slow down for fear?
Stagger for angst?
Stumble in agony?
Slip on the way to the gas chamber
in Osciwice which we call
Auschwitz?

The piles and piles of
ashen-colored canvas shoes
cry out in vain
our only answer:
tears and silence

Natasha

That little thing over her shoulder
radiating warmth—as if Texas in August
were a place needing heat!—
the fat-wrinkled arms the fat-wrinkled legs
chubby chin and cheeks the round belly
smelling like bread fresh out of the oven
fill the old woman with a need to protect
the small girl's future to conjure up good
fortunes for her unknown destiny to put layers
upon layers of kisses on her to shield her
from viruses and evil

ever so lightly the baby's breath blows down
grandmother's wrinkled neck wrinkled from too
much sun stiff from stooping over work from
bending low from giving in from saying yes to
all these men:
fathers preachers husbands teachers policemen
supervisors even sons!

yes she whispers you bet you are my darling
you are not going to stoop low I'll see to that
you are not going to be a yes-sir-girl you who
saves me from the daily drudgery you who are
sweet to me and innocent you who lifts me up
from my servitude you for whom this hard senseless

life is at long last worth living you who makes
me forget all the contempt which has been growing
in me for so many years like a cancer you for whom
I do not mind to continue the struggle just so
I survive just so I can hold you and kiss you
and feel your warm breath on my shoulder and
the softness of your chubby little body just
so that your life will be better than mine

now she starts singing ever so softly so as
not to wake up the precious load on her shoulder
hums a lullaby with her cracked voice but that's
alright—after all she had not been singing
for years and years

Counting Blessings

From one year to the next
you count your blessings in small
clay shards you throw them into the
basket woven from worry-hemp
by the Alabama-Cushetta tribes
or the Worpswede farmers

the wicker-work will outlive you
and probably your descendants because
the portion of good deeds meted out
and received here and everywhere seems
negligible:
Health
turning mellow though not wiser with age
a little saved-up laughter
the ability to weep
curiosity never-ending
an ounce of courage
the kind of nevertheless-courage
a come-hell-or-high-water-courage
a walking-cane courage
but courage nevertheless
and enjoyment of
kids
poetry
music
new ideas
fossils
and even some rather foolish things

Four Knights Opening

Sergei Task

Translated from the Russian by
Marian Schwartz

If life could be described in algebraic equations, with love and hate, passion and reason, ingenuousness and perfidy balancing each other out perfectly, then the story I want to tell you would be totally apropos, whereas at present it risks being relegated to the ranks of the merely curious, although I do hope this will make it none the worse—maybe even better—for what if not the curious can spice up the watery puree of the everyday. Of course, among my readers there are vegetarians as well, who prefer lenten verses and unseasoned novels, but these I would beg in advance not to trouble themselves and refer them to the literary disciples of Bragg.

Last fall I spent ten days at a small resort town in Abkhazia, in the home of a Greek woman I know, where besides me there were two other Muscovites, a young couple with a toddler from Leningrad, a Lithuanian woman with her granddaughter, and a big noisy family from I think Donetsk. I felt like part of a happening going on in that cramped yard, on the patch of ground between the well, the makeshift kitchen, and the henhouse. Here, under an overhang entwined with grapevines, stood a long table—the main prop and, simultaneously, the logical center of the improvisation played day in and day out, with variations, without pause or cease, with only a brief intermission of three or four hours, the hours when all cats are gray. The first, even before dawn, to cast his vote was the toddler behind the thin veneer screen that demonstrated yet again the conventional nature of the barrier artificially erected between Muscovites and Leningraders. Directly under the window of my small room in the half-basement where, in addition to me, two other devotees of sea bathing gladly took shelter, a stray mutt yelped irritably as he relived his proletarian origins with particular intensity in his dreams. The door to the annex opposite slammed—the miner dynasty was beginning its pilgrimage to holy places. Then a light blazed on in the kitchen: Grisha's wife, for whom all the sounds of the world had been drowned out once and for all in the howl of the giant pterodactyls that had chosen the Adler airport, put the coffeepot on the burner. A little later Grisha would get up and prime the well pump—an act of mercy (not for his wife, for us): maybe today we wouldn't hear their children, a girl and a boy, youthful terrorists with imaginations, carry out their next military sortie bombarding the peaceable nursery. Sudden animation in the henhouse could mean just one thing: the chicken god, whose superiority the rooster himself reluctantly acknowledged, had come out into the yard. I'll say! He was carrying a pail of choice millet mixed with something that doesn't have a name, and if it does, then an abstruse one, Latin, for the man ran a pharmacy, and his name was Fyodor, and he was married to Grisha's younger sister, who, as every chick knew, was expecting a child, otherwise why would the sewing machine be buzzing day in and out—Sofia was sewing a layette, that was quite obvious. But if Sofia didn't get up soon, then her other sister, Olga—she's the one who invited me to visit—she, I hear through my slumber, would have completely taken over in the kitchen. Meanwhile the nice Leningraders' fed toddler was stirring up trouble with the disgruntled mutt, who was at his wit's end in the morning trying to figure out where he'd buried his sugar bone the night before. The miner dynasty amicably began their ablution rite. In the annex, the six-year-old cutie was lisping something in Lithuanian. Car horns—that was Olga's parents, whose appearance the lightly sleeping grandmother blessed from the upper terrace, returning from a wedding.

That was how—more or less—the prologue to the day's action was played out, usually in several open areas, but primarily in the yard, and more specifically at the long table under the overhang, to the cackling of hens, the buzzing of the above mentioned sewing machine, and the unobtrusive muttering of the two televisions, one color and one black and white, that stood in front of the kitchen, one on top of the other, and fell silent long after midnight. But if I experienced the prologue somewhat vicariously, then the subsequent peripeteiae unfolded with my direct participation. I immediately became virtually the central, albeit passive, figure—because I was a male guest and, consequently, the ideal repository for food in the eyes of three women. Soon, though, my role expanded somewhat. I suspect that, willingly or not, I had come under attack from Grisha, who had given the grandmother an earful about how I wrote for Moscow magazines, whereas the only actual publication I could claim was a want ad in the classifieds ("Prepared to publish a story, 25 pages, in any magazine. No offers for foreign publications please. . . .") and how through me they could all go down in History. The cult of the printed word is obviously so highly developed among Abkhazian Greeks that I wasn't even all that surprised when two days later the yard filled with visitors. Neighbors came to get my help writing a letter to a minister suggesting that therapeutic mud baths at last be built next to their house, on the site of a perpetual puddle whose curative properties had been enjoyed by local inhabitants from time immemorial; under cover of night I was approached by a fussy man wearing an elastic headband who implored me in a theatrical whisper to inform certain authorities about the criminal activities of the local mafia, who secretly, in the foothills, behind a solid fence with an "M" on it, were testing explosive devices so powerful they made his skull crack; a shepherd came down from the mountains to stir up a case against a large flock of sheep that had refused to yield "hot" wool. I was sitting at the dining table, under the overhang, which bowed under its heavy load of grapevines, among steaming polenta, and lavash, and roast chickens, amid big bottles and small, huddled over petitions, complaints, and proposals. I'm not exaggerating: never before had I worked so intensively. The main thing was that never before had I tested myself in so many different genres simultaneously.

The grandmother took an active part in my work. This expressed itself in her recounting for each petitioner, in his presence, all there was to know about him, starting with the petty theft in his bare-belly past and ending with the escapades in his jeans present, and with such knowledge of the affair, moreover, that one could only guess what role she herself had played in this, shall we say, chamber play. She unrolled each compromising scroll with frightening thoroughness, and woe to whoever tried to make changes or clarifications in that list. For some reason the story has stuck in my memory about some distant relative who at his daughter's wedding put the gifts of money in a canvas bag and made sure to write down the exact sum and name of the giver so that he couldn't be caught unawares later by the organs of taxation.

So once when, I remember, I had just finished composing for a nervous young man a petition to the police to issue him a new passport or, at least, insert a page in the old, for the young man dreamed of marrying, and it turned out there was nowhere to note this seminal event in his life other than under "Military Service" since the preceding one, "Family Status," had been thickly tattooed by various registries in the country and there was no more space, on that quiet Sunday afternoon, yes, Sunday, because it was on Sundays that the clans joined in battle, the two branches of the Onufriadi family tree, which during the week would have no part of one another over the six-foot fence that separated their adjacent lots, a stone fence festooned with the yellow flowers of hate, and so on one such quiet Sunday, when the morning battles had abated and someone was getting first aid and often second aid immediately after from the chicken god, who, which in this case is more important, was also the head pharmacist, and until the evening skirmishes, for another two or three hours, in that pause when, exhausted by the midday heat, the fowl fell silent in the dusty branches of the persimmon and the very air breathed love and forgiveness, the grandmother asked me to bring her her book from the bedroom. I climbed to the upper terrace, walked through the living room with the real stucco molding, through the sisters' room, where a week's worth of panties was exhibited on the columns of their Akai sound system, and down a small hall past a bank of cans of Greek olives—a kind of Hellenic flourish that successfully enlivened the interior—and finally found myself in the grandmother's bedroom. Here reigned cleanliness and barracks-like order. I easily located the right book on the shelf and was already getting ready to leave when my eye fell on chess figures set out on the nightstand in the niche. I took a step closer to size up the position. The next move would checkmate White. But if . . .I moved a White pawn to h4. . .Still checkmate, just two moves later. I restored it to its previous position and left the bedroom.

.The grandmother was giving the nervous groom tea, but as soon as I handed her the dog-eared, coverless volume, she forgot all about her quest. She carefully took the well-read book, opened it at random, and began reading to herself, turning several pages at a time due to her obvious agitation. The silence was growing heavy; even the sewing machine bobbin whirred in fits and starts. The nervous groom undertook a concealed maneuver in the direction of the far corner of the table, having forgotten all about his ill-starred passport. Suddenly the grandmother tore herself away from the book and, aiming the bulging pupils in her sunken eye sockets at the groom, uttered, either in her own words or citing from memory: "In passionate love perfect happiness consists not so much in intimacy as in the final step toward it." The groom stiffened. The sewing machine fell silent. Even the henhouse experienced some confusion, or so it seemed to me. The grandmother sighed heavily and once again gave herself over to reading. Sofia, with exactly the same sigh, which was streaked not only with understanding but with tacit approval for the grandmother's hidden thoughts, turned the wheel on her Singer. A few minutes later the grandmother laid the book down on her knees, and her face became pensive.

"He's right," she said quietly. "A proud woman is most vexed by petty, inconsequential people, and she vents that vexation on noble souls." Distractedly, the grandmother straightened a folded under corner of the oilcloth. "Out of pride a woman is capable of marrying her idiot neighbor just to sting the idol of her heart that much more. Yes, yes, an idiot!" she repeated, convinced, turning for some reason toward the groom, who under her gaze progressed to a new stage—petrification.

"What kind of match is it you have set up in your room?" I tried to steer the conversation into a calmer channel. Sofia's eyes blazed in my direction, but I didn't

understand the signal and continued with the undue familiarity of a companion to the grandmother: "To tell the truth, in that situation I wouldn't risk playing White."
"Or Black," followed the scathing rebuke.
I bit my tongue.
"Perhaps I should go, yes?" the groom interjected, and he leaned all the way across the table for his passport.
No one stopped him.
"That's enough layette sewing already," said the grandmother as soon as she had shut the iron gate behind the visitor. "You'd think you were a hen hatching a dozen eggs. You ought to be sitting with your husband—look at the black eye Fyodor's got, and they're probably just about to start in again."
Sofia stood up abruptly, inasmuch as her eight-month belly permitted, and went into the big house. The grandmother and I were left to ourselves.
"Don't be offended at me, old lady that I am. When I think about that I'm not myself. Look, there's a gleam in your eye! All right, since that's the case, then listen. There you are looking at me, at my hands with their dark spots, and you're thinking—don't interrupt—and you're thinking the old lady is worse than a mortal sin. But do you know what I was called in my youth? Yelena the Beautiful. That's my photograph up there—take a look, take a look. Kostas stole a gold bracelet from his own mother—just to prove that he was prepared to do anything for me. And I wiped my feet on him...and a year later we were wed. Funny, yes? After that, Niko often came to see us. He came and sat—one hour, two, and then left without saying a word. My Kostas felt, if he wants to sit let him sit, Niko may have been only his cousin, but they were family, they had grown from a single tree. For me it was hell. I was even happy when they sat down at the chessboard, well, I thought, even so, that made it all easier. Easier! But to see him nearly every blessed day?! True, he

never started in with me about anything at all, I'm not going to lie. Even on my name day, when he brought me this very book, Stendhal, he didn't say anything, only when they left to play and I opened up to the bookmark and there it was underlined...just a minute"—she skimmed the dog-eared volume—"here: 'The sole medicine for jealousy consists, perhaps, in very close observation of the rival's happiness.' Yes..." She paused. "You know, I don't understand anything about chess, but once my husband, pleased with a victory over poor Niko (he almost always beat him), began to demonstrate certain moves to me on the board, I listened closely and toward the end asked: 'Then why did he lose to you?' My husband laughed for a long time and then said: 'He lost and he's going to keep on losing. Because he's as stubborn as a bull. I move a pawn and he moves a pawn, I move a bishop and he moves a bishop.' 'Can't you do that?' 'Yes! You can do anything! But I have my pace, you have to understand that! I have my pace!' Of course, I didn't understand anything, and he called me a fool and vowed never to talk to me about chess again." Only now did the grandmother notice the flies crawling brazenly over the jar of fig jam—for five years she had been trying unsuccessfully to get it past her insatiable grandchildren, and feed it to her great-grandchildren, *à la* the classic scene in the city park where the sharp sparrows steal the best crumbs out from under the noses of the pigeons for whom the crumbs were intended. The grandmother shooed the flies away and covered the jar with a plastic lid. "But he did"—she slowed down, as if checking her own memory—"he did speak to me about chess one more time. It was right before the war, five or six years must have passed."

"You mean to say that all those years they continued sparring over the chessboard?"

"You can imagine. When Kostas was hospitalized with suspected jaundice in the winter of '39, Niko's sister—you've seen her—at his request brought my dear husband messages to the hospital for two weeks. Only afterward did we realize that the only thing in those fat bundles was his next move."

"Yelena Kharlampiyevna," I reminded her, "you said that your husband spoke with you about chess one other time."

"Yes. After the match that remains on the board today. It was their last match." The grandmother's spine suddenly unbent, her eyes flashed, and for a moment I saw before me that same Yelena, Yelena the Beautiful, for whose sake stealing a gold bracelet from your mother was no sin. "He lost that time."

"Who? Niko?"

"My husband," she said almost indifferently, but, strangely, in her tone I sensed a note of triumph. "It was that rare instance when he lost. And how he lost!"

"Yes, it's a clever trap," I agreed.

"I'm not talking about any trap." The grandmother smiled. "They were playing, as people put it then, 'for stakes.' "

"You mean for money?"

"Not necessarily. For money, for a hunting rifle, for just about anything. The Onufriadis are a wealthy family."

"So what did your husband lose that time?" I asked, smiling in turn. "A cow?"

"Me," she said simply.

"Who?" I didn't understand.

"Me," she repeated.

I made an attempt to inflate a new smile, as if to say that we too are capable of recognizing a successful joke, but I don't think anything came of it.

"My husband also decided that Niko was joking," the grandmother continued as if nothing were amiss. "But he was so sure of himself that he accepted that audacious, that insulting bet. Afterward, trying to vindicate himself to me, he swore that he'd never even considered the thought of defeat. He knew Niko's passion for copying his moves so he settled on the Four Knights Opening—you see, I'm not such a fool anymore, I've learned something—he settled on it as entailing no risk. They'd already come across this opening, and Kostas as White had always checkmated Niko. I don't know whether it's true, but that's how my husband explained it to me later."

"So what happened?"

"No one knows. He was like a crazy man afterward. Shouting, tearing his hair. He wanted to kill me, himself, him. He'd even convinced himself that I'd set the whole thing up."

"But maybe Niko"—I stopped short, looking for the word—"maybe he didn't play completely above board?"

"You mean he cheated?" the grandmother clarified brutally. "Niko would never have done that!" For the first time she seemed to raise her voice, though she immediately took herself in hand. "Do you really think that my husband didn't check each move a hundred times? He sat over that devil's board until dark."

"And didn't find a mistake?"

"No."

I stole a look at the grandmother—old, completely gray, all in black, which made her seem almost incorporeal—and I couldn't ask the question that was on the tip of my tongue.

"I know what you want to ask. You want to ask whether my husband kept his bet? This is how I'd answer: he was too weak to send me off to something like that. He sprawled at my feet, hugging his gun, but when I got up from bed in the middle of the night and started dressing, he pretended to be asleep."

She fell silent, and so did I, even the two hens circled each other silently in mortal combat over a watermelon rind.

"But Niko, he didn't pretend," the grandmother continued. "No, he was not one for pretending. He was waiting for me. . . He was waiting to spurn me. Imagine! Niko turned me out! But my husband never found out about that, you understand, and before dawn they set out for White Cliffs. Have you been there?"

I had. The day I arrived the Leningraders took me with them to White Cliffs, which turned out to be stone cankers like dripped candle wax, right by the sea, about a half-hour's brisk walk. White Cliffs. . . a beautiful spot, no denying it. . . only desolate, especially that early.

"So I don't have to explain how far it is from here. But I heard it. A milky fog had just begun to disperse outside my window when I heard two shots, almost simultaneously."

I was expecting more, but the grandmother rose heavily from the bench and started clearing the dirty dishes.

"That's all?" burst out of me. I could tell how incredibly naive that sounded. Like a child who hears a sad story and expresses his objection to the cruel ending.

The grandmother shrugged her shoulders in reply.

"Help me clear the dishes away from the sink," was all she said. "They'll be starting soon." She craned her neck as if she were expecting a heavenly sign: lightning was about to strike the earth, like a golden staff, and then they could start.

And suddenly I realized! It was over her, over the grandmother, that they came together every Sunday! Of course! For forty-five years two branches of the Onufriadi family—grandfathers, fathers, and now even sons—bloodied each other over a once beautiful woman, each side hoping to vindicate, albeit half a century too late, their original claims, and nothing was more important for either than this. It meant restoring the original earthly order, when love was equivalent to itself and did not require adjustments for the size of a dowry or parental ties, when higher justice meant higher justice, only that and nothing more, when it was hardly appropriate to argue in the spirit of the modern thesis of the "survival of the fittest," and even if these latter-day Achilles and Patroclus—just as bellicose, just as naive—proved nothing to each other before the Second Coming, even so, every week they tried to demonstrate beyond a doubt to this proud old woman—and with her all mankind—the triumph of the spirit over pitiful matter.

"Have you gone deaf!" The grandmother was practically shoving plates into my face. "Why feed you men! Here, take these to the kitchen, dear."

I took the pile of sauce-encrusted dishes, chicken bones crunching between them, from her hands. When I had ferried everything to the kitchen, I was ordered to take Stendhal back. In the grandmother's bedroom I made a space for myself on the sagging couch, in a lap between two broken springs, and buried myself in the book. I should say that the book was pretty heavily penciled. One sentence was circled in red: "For a girl it is a much greater violation of her modesty to lie down in bed with a man whom she has seen twice in her life after saying a few words in Latin in a church than to be forced to yield to a man she has adored for two years." Lord, that's about them! was my first thought. And my second was that she hadn't circled that in red, he had! I hurried, afraid they would call me, the courier, back, I turned the well-worn, dog-eared pages, snatching certain bits at random, and suddenly a shock ran through me: I had reread a sentence three times, not believing my own eyes, but right then I heard steps on the terrace, and I started like a thief caught committing a crime, slipped Stendhal into a slit on the shelf, and left quickly.

On the terrace Grisha, dressed, had sprawled out to sleep. Evidently the mosquitoes had finally eaten him up in his room. Right before the sun set they "joined" once more. From my small room in the half-basement I heard little Niko, the legendary Niko's grand-nephew, invoke Christ the Savior to witness his opponent breaking the unwritten laws of fisticuffs; I heard Andrei Konstantinovich, Kostas' son, who had graciously opened the doors of his home to me, a stranger, loudly triumph after his crowning blow to the jaw; I heard them all. All but the grandmother's voice, but I didn't doubt one whit that during those sacred minutes she, as always, was sitting in her wicker chair on the upper terrace and from on high, like Pallas Athena, observing with interest the battle's progress. To the feeble support of my lamp, which the flies had turned into a candled quail's egg, I hastened to write down the astonishing tale. The grandmother, I felt, had omitted something important. But what? Maybe she didn't know herself. Didn't know? But what about the sentence from Stendhal? Couldn't that sentence, in fact, have escaped her notice, even though it was underlined? And that opening. . . four knights. . .why did it trouble me so? Her husband, she said, had found no mistake, had checked each move a hundred times and hadn't found. . . Actually though, why should I believe her husband? Niko's win was no accident, that's clear, the stakes were too high for that, and that meant. . . Here the thread of my reasoning broke time after time. I had to go out and recreate the position, that's what. And play it out from there. Granted, with my chess erudition I wasn't going to play it out very far. No matter. I'd go back to Moscow and sort it out there. Yes, I honestly admit, I was quite obsessed by then, and when an idea gets hold of me, I can hang the moon in ribbons.

I apologize in advance for rattling off how imperceptibly those last days by the sea passed for me, how I took the grandmother's tkemali home with me, and, oh yes, her divine fig jam, how I didn't have a return ticket and Grisha's wife Tanya got me an "overflow" flight, favor for favor, after all I'd written a letter to Aeroflot for the girls on duty in which I wrote something histrionic about how they were going deaf on the airstrip and weren't even getting any extra compensation for it. Not that all this was unimportant, but right now, this minute, I, like you too, reader, doubtless, was already there, in Moscow, where, one would like to believe, the solution to this bizarre story awaited us.

The day after I flew into Moscow, on Tuesday, I called the Central Chess Club and was distressed to hear that the library was only open evenings. In order to make the time pass more quickly, I saw a trashy movie, ate lunch twice—on grounds of nerves (and was still hungry)—and roamed the city. By four o'clock on the button I was at the cozy building on Gogol Boulevard. In the library they gave me literature on the theory of openings, a box of wooden chess pieces, and a folding board. In less than an hour I had found what I was looking for. Quite agitated, I played out the fatal match that had ended in two shots. It turned out that in 1936 the newspaper *Evening Moscow* had chosen this opening for a match with its readers. Up to the eleventh move Black copied White's moves exactly. Further continuation of this symmetry quickly threatened the readers with checkmate, so on White's eleventh move Qd2 they moved the bishop to f3, taking the knight. But that didn't save them either and on the twentieth move they conceded defeat.

Did Niko Onufriadi know about this curious match? I don't think I would be wrong if I answered in the affirmative. But after all, he, Niko, had won with Black! Yes, won... after losing many times, knowingly following the false lead pursued by *Evening Moscow's* readers. Yes, over and over again, he lost to his cousin and rival, laying the groundwork for the principal match of his life. And when the decisive moment came, he played the eleventh move in a new way—he moved to check with his knight to f3. Lulled by easy victories, suspecting nothing, his rival made his following moves essentially under his dictate. On the fourteenth move Niko modestly moved his king to the corner of the board . . . and White was trapped! After Kt:f6 followed Rd8. Mate! A belated attempt to open a "window" to the White king also, as I had been convinced even then, in the grandmother's bedroom, led to mate. Well well! Kostas' eyes must have popped out of his head. I wouldn't have been surprised if he'd had a stroke.

You ask: what makes me think Niko had to have known about that match? And if he did, then what devil made him play giveaway with his rival for so long? Stop! Why don't we ask ourselves *how* long? If my memory serves me well, between Kostas' first and last attempts to familiarize his wife with the ancient game five or six years passed, the last one of these, shall we say, pre-duel conversations taking place right before the war. Consequently. . . Don't rush, this requires absolute precision. I set out for the public library and in the card file under "Stendhal, Henri Beyle," I looked for the same volume from the fifteen-volume collected works he'd given to Yelena the Beautiful. The 1935 edition! Good for you, old woman, everything checks out—six years. So that's when this maniac got the idea for his bizarre plan! I'm talking about that sentence in Stendhal that so astonished me.

So, it was then, in '35, that Niko was frequenting his cousin's house. I don't think he had a precise plan of action at first. I think he got the idea of adopting "mirror" chess as his ally from the comment in *Evening Moscow*. An ingenious plan, by the way. How else, I ask you, could you program your rival for the desired result? Oh, I didn't believe in those countless losses of his from the very beginning! Anyone Beautiful Yelena had loved for fifty years was worth her weight in gold. She did love him, she did! "He was so pleased with his victory over poor Niko," she had said. That word, "poor," probably told him more than she'd intended. The sly dog, he had let himself be beaten so often in this game of cat and mouse that toward the end he risked losing the ways of the hunter. Even more amazing, though, was his long-suffering patience. To come to the house of someone who belonged to another every day for six years and, without giving yourself away, lose to a conceited fool time and again—you'll agree, not everyone is capable of that. I figured in my head: in six years they must have played about fifteen hundred matches. The openings varied, naturally, however by all accounts up to a specific moment he always mirrored the moves of his opponent, passing it off as his aberration, or "stubbornness," as Kostas assumed, but in actual fact by degrees accustoming the latter to the idea that he would go on like that forever. In this sea of matches the Four Knights Opening must have come up more than once (after all, Kostas himself admitted as much!). Amazingly, though, Niko passed up his chance over and over again. He had no right to take the risk! And he suggested his astonishing bet, of course, not *before* the start of their decisive match but *after,* when their knights, White and Black, were rushing at each other, foaming at the mouth, and everything became immediately clear, and both weapons shot soundlessly, so that a little later, at dawn, the echo could reverberate at White Cliffs. But then why, we ask ourselves, having borne his cross and reached the threshold of bliss, didn't he take that last step? That riddle, I'm afraid, is beyond me.

  My story is drawing to a close. I'm looking back over the first pages and I can't shake a certain ambivalence: if the main, love-chess *sujet* has been written more or less straightforwardly and convincingly, then

everything leading up to it seems to fall short: a strange intonation creeps into the description of the household arrangement, sentences are at times heavy and airless, the humor, as they say, of the Evil One. What's to be done? There is nothing more false in art than being true to life.
  I cannot part with my reader on this sad note. The match has been played, the pieces are returning to their starting positions. What are we to do? I roamed aimlessly in the rain and thought about my beautiful Greek lady. I also felt like sacrificing something for her, if not my life then . . . then . . . I went to Kuznetsky Bridge, scouted around among the black market dealers, and the next day had in hand, for a mere 500 percent markup, a paperback of ambiguous color with an equally ambiguous sketch depicting either a breaking adipose heart or a time bomb toward which the foxfire of passion was inexorably stealing up a safety fuse. It was Stendhal. I sent the grandmother the book, having inserted a bookmark. She would open Stendhal and surely turn immediately to the sentence underlined in red: "A woman can be won, like a chess match."

  Having come to a full stop, I surveyed the field of battle one last time. Suddenly a shock ran through me. What blindness! All it took for White to escape checkmate was to play: 15. Rfcl Rg8+ 16. Kf1 Bg2+ 17. Kel. Kostas *could have* saved himself! My poor hero—your dream nearly burst, like a balloon. But the story has already been written. I'm happy I gave you this illusion, albeit at the expense of my own mistake.

Faux Pas
Origins of the Social Blunder in Human Civilization

Skye Kathleen Moody

Author's Note: *The* faux pas, *or false step, is a globally accepted term identifying a social error, breach of tact or manners, or any act committed against convention or propriety. Human cultures abound in* faux pas, *though their nature often differs from one culture to the other.* Faux pas, *whether committed out of ignorance or sheer laziness, can bring embarrassment and even grave consequences to bear on the guilty party.* Faux pas *may be minor,* (petit faux pas), *or* faux pas *may be grand (e.g., atrocity); few are overlooked.*

The earliest record of the *faux pas* appears in the *Forgotten Books of Eden:* "Wherefore God did not put Adam there (south of Eden), lest he should smell the sweet smell of those trees, forget his transgressions *(faux pas)*, and find consolation for what he had done, and not be cleansed..."

With these words, the spirit of the *faux pas* sprang to life on Earth. Unfortunately, the record does not describe the substance of the *faux pas* Adam committed in Eden, a transgression so serious that Adam's God banished him from Eden to an area where he might be "cleansed." We do not even know if Adam's transgression was of a truly social nature, but since it involved, at least peripherally, the only other human in Eden—Eve—and since God's punishment took the form of social banishment for both Adam and Eve, we may assume Adam committed some sort of *social blunder.*

Adam's blunder might have been quite minor, a *petit faux pas,* or might have registered on a grander scale, no one knows for certain; thus, the definition of the *faux pas* and the appropriate penance for social blundering have suffered from vagueness since the first false step in Eden. This vagueness has itself been incorporated into the *faux pas* tradition: today the party injured by another's *faux pas* (for there must always be an injured party) may independently judge the nature and gravity of the blunderer's insult and decide upon a course of punishment. This vagueness places the oft bewildered transgressor at the very mercy of the injured party, and since the time of Adam and Eve, a strong retaliatory reaction to the faux pas has been the global tendency.

Over the course of history, *faux pas* of monumental significance (though never as great as Adam's) have been recorded. Atrocities have been committed by governments against their citizens, by governments against citizens of other nations, by religion against science and science against religion, by technology against humankind and by humankind against its several tongues. The definition of a social transgression is so all-encompassing and frustratingly vague that citing history's most serious *faux pas* (after Adam's) becomes a monumental task. An idle shuffle through the Durant collection turns up thousands of spectacular examples of the atrocity and other grand *faux pas.* Yet world history is notably lacking in records of the *petit faux pas,* presumably because the tendency of historical figures is to do nothing less than grand.

Some confusion has arisen in the past over whether a single human could commit a *faux pas* grand enough to outrage the entire world. The question harks back to Eden and the case of Adam; but Adam lived in lonely times void of large population centers which might have taken mass offense at his transgression. (Though beasts proliferated in Eden, wildlife is notorious for ignoring *faux pas* altogether.) But Adam had Eve, the only other human around, and reportedly the Temptress who tripped him up. And Adam had God, Who, records show, was the single Injured Party. Thus, while Adam committed the greatest *faux pas* ever known (its exact nature still somewhat of a niggling mystery), he in fact transgressed against but One Individual.

As Earth's population inevitably swelled, a sort of competition arose: Who could outrage the entire world? The grand *faux pas* became fashionable in certain elite circles, notably among kings and dictators, wealthy liberal industrialists, feckless politicians and flamboyant couture designers. Of this hierarchy of offenders, the individual best known for committing a grand *faux pas* (of the atrocity order) was Adolph Hitler. Hitler belonged to the school of social fascism, a cult still in existence today. Hitler-style fascists, though numbering a few powerful cowards, hold that crimes of mass murder and violence may be dismissed when committed under the thin guise of "national interest," or "privilege of the ruling class."

Since Hitler committed suicide, one can only speculate what punishment might have been brought to bear against him for the commission of atrocities. As in the case of most atrocities, the victims did not survive to mete out justice. Hitler's cerebral depravity combined with the evil nature of his deeds marks him forever as civilization's most feared reflection of its own darkest side. Hitler remains today the world's most glaring example of the grand *faux pas* as atrocity.

On the brighter side of the many-faceted social blunder, the artist Salvador Dali committed what is known as a cultural *faux pas*. By a quirk of Nature, Dali perceived the world and its objects as fluid matter; the transference of his mental images to sundry *objets d'art* outraged large segments of civilization and sparked a revolution in the visual arts. While not the sole perpetrator of surrealism, Dali nevertheless succeeded more than any other artist in causing the world to drip. Dali's followers encourage asymmetrical art forms, cultural *faux pas*, if you will, which stimulate the human neo-cortex. Why, they argue, must life on Earth be depicted in uniform cubes and squares, triangles and conical circularities, when in fact, as Dali so gloriously illustrated, much of the population sees things oozing? Dali's grand *faux pas* has been held aloft as a positive and even sensually stimulating artistic triumph. Dali's *faux pas* is one example of social transgression which outrages some while inspiring another crowd. Dali, then, represents the complexities in the definition of the *faux pas*.

From Eden to the present day no single individual has yet succeeded in committing a *faux pas* which outraged the entire global community, but the contest rages forth. Steeped in transgressional fantasies a handful of contenders both in politics and the arts employ various high-tech inventions and twisted vision in an effort to do what Adam did on a grander scale. (A half hour session with MTV or fifteen minutes with CNN amply illustrates this point.) The remainder of the population, meanwhile, is content to commit *petit faux pas* galore.

One ancient school of *faux pas* held that where little false steps abound no mortal sin dare trod. Thus by small steps would the world be saved. Propriety, according to this theory, is preserved by the frequent commission of *petit faux pas*. This school has revived and today enjoys a rather large and gullible following. As we shall see, there are inherent dangers in this theory of accumulative *faux pas*.

The school of cultural fascism, small in numbers today, is a splinter group of the *faux pas* purists. Though not always pro-violence, as in the case of cultural fascism, the purists contend that venial transgression breeds its mortal heir, and that **all forms of *faux pas* must be avoided at any cost.** These bold words reveal the devious twist in their logic. Largely comprised of fanatics who strive ever towards what they are wont to term a "total clear," the purists believe that God all along intended for Adam and the Temptress to conduct themselves in Eden in a manner of unblemished perfection and blissful ignorance. (Whether or not God confused Adam and the T with the Good Angels is not known, and some *faux pas* experts argue for Lucifer as the Original Transgressor. But since Lucifer was not from Eden, not even from Earth, though later exiled there, this academic question escapes relevance in the study of the human *faux pas*.)

The anti-*faux pas* school argues that social transgression must be avoided, and when committed, ought to be harshly punished. When studying the social behavior of the anti-*faux pas* group (a spinoff, incidentally, from the *faux pas* purists) an interesting pattern emerges, raising serious objections to the school itself: many anti-*faux pas* purists have actually committed grand *faux pas* in secret! The trick phrase "must be avoided at any cost" is the key which unlocks the abyss of this school's hypocrisy. Among anti-*faux pas* ranks one observes individuals from every walk of life, and there derives from this diverse crowd a strong tendency towards cultural fascism. These "total clear" guruvian channelists, more than any other humans on Earth today, are to be avoided.

Finally, a more tolerant attitude exists towards the *faux pas*, that of the blithe spirit school (variously described as idealists, romantics, willowheads, naifs, and even Penguinesque—God only knows what that is all about, and we choose not to speculate). These individuals, springing from every race, class, cultural and educational background, hold that faux pas, *petit* and grand, have always been and will continue to be an integral quirk in human civilization's crazy-quilt nature. Blithe spirits posit a unique twist on the human quirk. While accepting that Adam, if he existed, might indeed have socially transgressed against his God's will, these Tolerant Souls point to the abundance of snakes and apples in Eden (trans.: Earth) and to God's (presumably theirs and Adam's is the Same) forgiving Nature, interpreting His punishment of Adam in a refreshing light: God merely told Adam and the Minx to clear out of town until they could learn to behave in a civilized manner (evolution being a constant progression towards this goal). The descendants of Adam and Co. are still learning how to play it in Rome, and once they have down pat the knack of propitious behavior, the Kingdom will be wide open for business. *Faux pas,* blithe spirits maintain, are little steps backwards or sideways, in any case, practically harmless steps in the wrong direction which often trod upon the sensitive peds of other sojourners.

The victim of a *faux pas*, according to the b.s. philosophy, shows wisdom in forgiveness (while never tolerating atrocity) and encourages learning from others' transgressions, if rarely from one's own. Gradually, as the population learns to navigate one another's little false steps (and some of the grander gaffes), civilization will find itself dancing gracefully down various primrose paths all perfectly acceptable since all lead to the same destination, be it via Rome, the City of God, Seventh Heaven (read: Nirvana, Upper Eden, Montecarlo), the grave, or simply Tulsa. This *faux pas* tolerance finds wide acceptance in contemporary cross-cultural climates, as one social group pollinates another, and so on.

Today, only a few individuals still compete with Adam, and they are regarded as civilization's lowest lot. But those who, like Adam, fall into temptation (Minx or no Minx) and subsequently repent are forgiven—even if they never so much as blushed during the indiscretion. Thus, in contemporary civilization's eyes, to sum up the *faux pas:* The world is a crooked tango. False steps abound. The worst *faux pas* is committing no *faux pas* at all. *Petit faux pas* may be Silently Borne or may be sneered at; there is no middle ground. Crimes of atrocious magnitude have been altogether deleted from the modern day definition of the *faux pas*. Today, grand *faux pas* are defined more on the scale of big blunders, e.g., passing gas in a public place (illegal in the City of San Diego, less contentious elsewhere). A slip of the scalpel, a slip of the networkian tongue, taking pets to wedding ceremonies (unless invited), entering a roomful of conservatives stark naked, are all examples of what makes a grand *faux pas* today.

Public figures and surgeons are strictly prohibited from committing grand *faux pas*, but may indulge in *petit faux pas* now and then for purposes of attracting attention to themselves at parties. Scientists and True Artists are granted sweeping license to toy with *faux pas*; impostors are cast out. (Was Adam an impostor?) All categories of travelers (tourists, ambassadors, voyeurs, expats, lemmings, etc.) are permitted two *petit* cultural *faux pas* per country visited, as long as their airport taxes are paid. Scholars in all fields may err prolifically, except in bold print with footnotes. News anchors may slip only on the weather report. The rest of the world's citizens are free to gaffe to their hearts' desire, within the broad scope of *petit faux pas* and excepting smoking in public areas. This is comforting news.

Four Faux Pas & Why To Avoid Them

Margin of Hydra

Note: *Excerpted with the author's permission from* The Alien's Guide to Planet Earth, *by Margin of Hydra.* © *1995*

Committing a *faux pas* today is generally less serious than in past eras. However, a proper demeanor is always preferred and certainly one should strive toward it. The wheels of tradition are constantly greased by a revolution over propriety's foggy path, and what was once considered a social blunder now is frequently acceptable behavior. One just never knows for sure. Furthermore, in spite of the trend to tolerance pointed out in Moody's laborious tome, it is wise to remember that no matter how petty, a social blunder may embarrass all parties involved and might earn the transgressor insult, derision, a slap on the cheek or worse.

Even today, certain *faux pas* can result in punishment by death. While kings and presidents frequently commit grand *faux pas en masse* with no grave consequences to themselves, the unprotected and innocent alien is not so privileged. Anyone might commit a social blunder unknowingly; anyone, even an alien, can learn to avoid them. Following are four of Earth's least described but most serious *faux pas*. These acts, motions, gestures, verbal utterings and visual innuendoes should be scrupulously avoided:

#1 Indiscreet Landings

It is a well known fact that aliens are wont to land anywhere on Earth that suits their fancies. Some aliens pay for this indulgent carelessness. A good example is the first landing of the Zinn Collective at the prehistoric birthday party thrown for King Neptune by the Society of Whales.

The Zinns, on their first visit to Earth, put down at 35° latitude, 123° longitude, plunging some fourteen hundred meters into calm Pacific waters off the coast of Southern California. Their time of arrival: approximately 3:12 p.m., on the afternoon of 1,001 B.C., August 1st.

Anyone with a whit of common sense knows that this date marks King Neptune's birthday. This day of celebration finds the Pacific Ocean transformed into a virtual carnival, replete with decorated flotsam and grandly executed parades. Schools out on holiday, great masses of fish can be expected to crowd along the review stands for close-up views. Oyster beds are abandoned for the day, as oysters join in the festivities, along with clams, mussels, most anemones and mollusks. (Warning: Sea urchins operate among the spectator crowds, skillfully pickpocketing innocent parade-goers.) The carnival atmosphere reaches its climax at approximately 3:13 p.m. (PDT), and this fact is what the Zinn Collective failed to take into consideration when they put down.

The Zinn ship plunged squarely into King Neptune's lap, just as the Whale Society was presenting His Highness' birthday cake. You can imagine the chaos that resulted. The Zinns were immediately apprehended and delivered to the King's dungeon. There the Zinns languished in kelp-infested cells for nearly two hundred years. When finally they were released, King Neptune banished the Zinns with a strict warning, *viz.*, never to pollute his waters again. Thus the Zinns were permanently banished from the Pacific Ocean. This unfortunate fact glares when reading the Zinn's World Grammar; it lacks the undersea languages so desperately needed to decode the ways of denizens of the deep.

Zinn might have avoided this *faux pas* had the collective just taken a few minutes to evaluate their landing site and time of arrival before putting down.

Indiscreet landings not only cause embarrassment, they also impede the course of progress. Watch your latitudes and longitudes, and don't forget to refer to the Intergalactic Social Calendar when planning an Earth landing.

#2 Wrong Way Corrigan

One of the most annoying *faux pas* is that of the careless alien who hasn't studied Earthmaps carefully. I know of one particularly terrible incident, involving an alien whose name I won't mention, who was looking for the Holland Tunnel. This alien thought (stupidly) that the Holland Tunnel was located at 53º latitude, 04º longitude, in the City of Amsterdam. He put down in the middle of an operating room at Amsterdam Royal Hospital, precisely at the moment of the birth of a baby human. When he landed, he landed cheek to jowl with the newborn.

The attending physician noticed our friend the alien, and a sort of annoyed trepidation crossed his expression. He muttered to the attending nurses, "It's twins, by golly! I didn't expect twins."

"Don't be silly, Doctor," quipped one of the nurses. "That thing (meaning, presumably, our friend) isn't an infant human. Why, it looks . . . it looks like something from outer space! Doctor, I think Mrs. Van der horst has produced an alien!"

"Who's being silly, Nurse," snapped the doctor. He reached over and plucked the alien from where he cowered very close to this Mrs. Van der horst's warm and comforting presence. The doctor held the alien up to strong light and examined him in every respect.

"I say," mused the doctor to his nurses, "this one *is* an ugly little thing. Should we throw him out with the bathwater and just not tell Mrs. Van der horst about him?"

Just then, the alien squeaked, "Which way to the Holland Tunnel?"

Horrified at this question, the doctor raised a large and calloused hand and smacked the alien square across the backside, causing a frightful cry to elicit from the alien's mouth.

"Oh dear, Doctor," moaned one of the nurses. "He doesn't sound at all like a human baby."

The first born of Mrs. Van der horst's meanwhile suckled peacefully on his mother's breast. Mrs. Van der horst sighed and opened her eyes. "What's that?!" she cried suddenly, gesturing at the alien held high by the doctor.

"It's, er, ah . . . that is, Mrs. Van der horst, you are the mother of twin boys. Both healthy, though one appears slightly, shall I say, dubious about entering the world. You see how he cowers in my palm."

Mrs. Van der horst studied the infant even now guzzling her breast. She studied the other "infant" held aloft by doctor's deft and courageous hand. She smiled and reached out to the cowering alien.

"Give him here," she said. "I have two of these things, you know."

Reluctantly, the doctor handed the alien over to Mrs. Van der horst. She placed him beside the human infant, guiding the alien's mouth gently toward a milk valve.

"There, ducky," smiled Mrs. Van der horst. "Now what shall I name you two?"

She finally settled on Piet and Albert, naming the first infant son after her ex-husband, and the second (you-know-who) after Albert Drente, the grocer's delivery boy.

Today, Albert Van der horst is a respected barrister and collector of Hank Williams memorabilia. No one knows his true identity, nor does anyone really care. But don't mistake Albert's success for true happiness. Back home on his planet, the alien had another half and several offlings. His selfishness in refusing to return to them was only part of what caused his melancholia. Albert, the alien, could never find a single person in Amsterdam who had heard of the Holland Tunnel, let alone tell him how to find it. Furthermore, Albert was constantly haunted by his deceitful act of portraying twin to Piet. So you can be sure this alien regretted in his heart his own failure to consult Earthmaps before going off half-cocked looking for the Holland Tunnel.

We'll hear more about Albert the alien in later installments. Should you come to Earth and desire to get in touch with Albert, to learn firsthand what it's like to get lost on Earth, forget it. Albert has become so humanized that he avoids aliens when he meets them in the street, and will never admit his true identity. Later on, I'll tell you what happened to Mrs. Van der horst.

#3 Tempting Crocodiles

It was last winter, I recall, when I met Nood. She came from Hexus, and was therefore stupid and bumbling in the fine art of love. Nood joined my safari into the depths of Bwanaland, and she never came away from there.

Bwanaland is located at approximately 37º longitude, 0º latitude, its capitol being the Mt. Kenya Safari Club. Bwanaland is populated mostly by passionate birds, deadly insects—the female mosquito thrives there—cold reptiles and fierce mammals of the dual-brained category. (Humans, as you know, have triunal brain structures.) Very few humans inhabit Bwanaland. Even so, some of these humans imagine themselves superior to other resident creatures, hence the designation Bwanaland.

Nood came to Bwanaland with only one idea in her Hexian mind. She wanted to study the habits of the crocodile. Now, Nood was an attractive alien, too attractive for her own good. When our expedition arrived at the Mt. Kenya Safari Club, we were immediately greeted by the lascivious stares of men dressed up as penguins. That very first evening, Nood, who had changed into the formal wear required in the club's dining room, stunned everyone to adoring silence when she wafted in wrapped in the evilest black dress, long slits up the sides, and an absolutely marvelous fit across the derriére. (Nood was posing as a female human, I forgot to mention.) She joined our table, but soon as she sat down, the waiter came floating over with a note for Nood. This is what it said:

> *My Dear Lovely Lady,*
> *Never before have my eyes rested upon such beauty as yours. It is possible you come from another planet, from another space and time?*

(This of course caused a bit of anxiety at our table. But on gazing round the dining room, I felt certain the author of the love letter had merely swooned allegorically. He swooned on:)

> Rumors abound around the club that you, dear Lady, are intensely interested in the habits of the crocodile. And so I am offering you the opportunity to study the biggest crocodile in Bwanaland. Meet me at the entrance to Cottage 12 at ten o'clock tonight, and I shall be honored to show you my crocodile.
>
> *In profound awe,*
>
> *Reginald Petrie*

Nood, of course, sought my advice concerning the...tryst. I strongly advised her against meeting this Reginald Petrie, and, employing every digit on both hands, I ticked off the reasons why. I needn't recount them, and the reader can probably guess at least half of them anyway. Suffice to say, Nood ignored my good advice, and at ten o'clock that very evening stole away from the revelry in the lodge and slipped along the garden path to Cottage 12.

Nood found the male, Reginald, waiting for her. He was tall for a human, perhaps fifteen feet, and his tuxedo strained around the collar and shirt studs. Nevertheless, Nood perceived Reginald as totally captivating, the most alluring man she'd ever encountered.

What happened that night in Cottage 12 is really none of our business. Suffice to say, the Southern Cross beamed down upon that lovenest as brightly as laser beams at war. Nood followed Reginald into the cottage and that is all we feel we should report about this strange affair of the night.

Next morning, Nood came swooning to the breakfast table and refused a second helping of toast and marmalade just like that.

"Nood," I said, annoyed, "Where are your good manners? Don't you know these Bwanians expect guests to put away at least two helpings of their delicious homemade toast? Do you wish to offend our gracious host, the manager, Mr. Hoarau?"

"I simply can't eat a thing," the little tramp swooned. "My appetite seems to have gone the way of blue bongos and purple tatwiddles."

"What is a tatwiddle?" I asked, my annoyance growing by the millisecond.

"An extinct bird which once infested the forests of my homeland planet. They became purple when the intergalactic climatologists sprayed our homeland with Innocence Powder."

As she spoke, Nood's eyes wandered about the dining room. She was searching, I felt positive, for her *amor* of the previous night.

"Why did they spray Hexus?" I asked her, knowing very well the answer to the question, but hoping to distract Nood from her annoying eye exercises.

"You know why," she said, and then her eyes rested at last upon me. "Why Margin!" she sang in her mellifluous way, "I do believe you're jealous of Reginald!"

There was no use denying the bald fact. I bit into a piece of toast and avoided looking into her vermilion eyes. Just then, that giant of a gigolo swaggered into the dining room and straight over to our private table.

"May I join you for breakfast?" he asked nervily.

I stood up and, pleading apologies, told the two of them I was late for a game drive. They didn't seem at all concerned and, in fact, this Reginald slipped into my seat as if he owned it. From a distance, no further than a blue bongo length, I watched as this Reginald buttered hot toast, spread it thick with marmalade and fed it to Nood.

She'd consumed ten pieces before I stopped counting.

What was the use? Nood had fallen in love with Reginald Petrie and so voluminously had he filled her heart and stomach that not even a dark chamber had been reserved for me. I turned and walked out of the dining room, hoping my heartbroken condition might be salved by a lusty game drive through the bush. I should never have deserted Nood at that moment, but the ultimate responsibility for what happened next must be carried by Nood. She, after all, was playing the vixen.

The accounts of what happened next are many and contradictory in some respects. What we know for certain is that Reginald Petrie suggested to Nood that they carry a plate of toast down to the river to feed the crocodiles. Nood apparently agreed to this plan of action, gathered up a full plate of toast and followed Reginald down to the riverbanks.

Nood was never seen again. But Mr. Hoarau, the manager of Mt. Kenya Safari Club, claims to have heard Nood's distinctive chimes crying out for help. When the hunters reached the riverbank, the only sign of Reginald and Nood was an empty toast platter and a very long tuxedo floating on the murky waters.

What Nood chose to do with her life was her own business, of course. By all accounts, it seems she changed her mind at the very last minute, but then it was too late. Her *petit faux pas, viz.*, tempting a crocodile, resulted in a fate worse than . . . well, than becoming a safari bush guide, for example. Or the wife of one.

The most unpleasant result of Nood's *faux pas*, though, was what her behavior did to the alien credibility factor. By refusing to conduct herself as a lady in the sacred environs of the Mt. Kenya Safari Club, Nood both appalled and disgusted polite society. From the evil black dress with its tight derriére to her antics in Cottage 12, Nood proved that even the alien is capable of behaving like a common tramp. For days afterward, she was the talk of the club, and I thanked my lucky stars Nood had not been revealed to Bwanians in her true identity.

Don't disgrace your fellow aliens—and yourself—by tempting crocodiles.

#4 Cyberphelia Syndrome

Mrs. Pension lives in a duplex at seashore on the New Zealand coast. Mrs. Pension is eighty-nine years old, has rheumatism and two mongrel dogs named Flip and Flap. Mrs. Pension also owns a personal computer and subscribes to various networks, including Flotsam-scan and Cybertechs. Mrs. Pension is a closet Cyberpheliac.

Imagine her surprise when a certain alien, whose name I shouldn't mention, turned up on her doorstep one day and demanded to borrow her personal computer.

"I'm on line," snapped Mrs. Pension. "You've a nerve dropping in like this and asking me to turn over my juice to the likes of you." Then she snorted, "You ain't from New Zealand, boy, that's clear as the breast on your face."

Then Mrs. Pension paused and thought over what she'd just said. She studied her visitor more closely, rubbing a hand across her whiskered chin as she did so.

"Young. . .er. . .man," she said suspiciously, "Where are you from?"

This alien, who lacked even the slightest trace of good sense, replied, "I'm from the Planet Hexus, ma'am. I've lost contact with my ship, and would be obliged if you could loan me your computer. Just for a few minutes. So I can contact my ship."

"Bother!" cried Mrs. Pension hotly. "I don't believe a word of it. If you're lost, why don't you go over to the police station? It's right next door to the post." She slammed the door in the alien's countenance.

He was a persistent little alien. Climbing up onto the duplex's roof, he located the chimney leading to Mrs. Pension's quarters, and before Mrs. Pension could say

"Cyberphelia," the alien had landed with a thud on her kitchen hearth. Mrs. Pension came after him with a long broom.

"Here now, get out I say!" She swept and swept at the alien, but he was very quick on his rotors and scurried under the computer console where she could not reach him with the broom. She made a sharp sound with her tongue and the roof of her mouth. She put the broom away and returned to her video console.

She had no sooner found her place in the Cybertechs network than the alien sprang out from under the console table and frightened her nearly to death.

"Who *are* you?" cried Mrs. Pension. "And *what* do you want?"

"I told you already," said the stupid alien. "Just let me use your computer for ten minutes. That's all I ask."

"Oh, go ahead," sighed Mrs. Pension. "It's no use anyway. I can't concentrate as long as you're here getting in my hair."

Ten minutes later, the alien had located his ship. But although he might have been grateful to Mrs. Pension and graciously acknowledged her generosity, the ingrate lingered in the graphics mode.

"Here, here," said Mrs. Pension angrily. "You're messing up my Cybertechs connection! What are you doing in the graphics mode?"

"Just fooling around," said the selfish outsider.

"Well, you'll get yourself into trouble doing that," muttered Mrs. Pension. She went off to the sewing room and left the alien at the video console.

For perhaps an hour the greedy alien played with Mrs. Pension's personal computer. It was not until near dusk that he realized he was late for the rendezvous with his ship. Scampering down the computer's keyboard, he accidentally tripped the graphics mode plunger.

Beastly sounds roared from the console. The alien cried out and rotored towards the door, attempting to escape the terrible images now escaping from Mrs. Pension's computer. But soon followed on the alien's proverbial heels two fluffy creatures which had leaped off the video screen. These terrible ginger colored beasts wore blue satin ribbons around their fat necks. Their teeth were Scrabble chips, but pointed. Their eyes were blood red beams. Their tongues lolled from foaming mouths, and both had rotten, fetid breath. The alien ran as fast as he could, but the creatures ran faster.
  I don't know which one ate him. Flip or Flap.

A Cellblock Mass

Raymond A. Schroth, S.J.

Note: *This is a chapter from a novel,* The Fall Semester, *which takes place at St. Jude's College, a small Catholic college in the Midwest. Father Hope is an English professor in his thirties.*

The gust of a November Sunday morning snow stung John Hope's face and bit the knuckles of the hand clutching his briefcase as, head down, leaning into the wind, with Susan Cahill and Rick Random in tow, he pushed his way across the parking lot of the Smoketown county prison.

It was 7 a.m., daylight had barely broken through the snowstorm, and saying this prison mass had not been John's idea. But the prison mass was an apostolate of the St. Jude's College Fathers' Hall which also brought in a weekly stipend of thirty dollars from the diocesan office of social concern. Father Detweiler, who usually serviced the prison, had flown to his sister's home in the Virgin Islands and had left a note on the community board asking for a volunteer. John had never been inside a jail, except once when, as a seminarian teaching high school, he visited a student who had raped and dismembered a seven-year-old girl. "I don't know what I'm doing here, Mr. Hope," the boy had said. "I think they're just making the whole thing up."

So John volunteered—partly because no one else had, and partly to ingratiate himself with the fathers in Fathers' Hall who, he had heard, resented the time he spent with students. At the moment, he was now operating on four hours sleep—having already concelebrated the Saturday night 1 a.m. mass with his partner Harold, where the gospel had been Matthew 25:1-13, the story of the "wise and foolish bridesmaids" (also translated as "virgins" and "maidens"), five of whom had wisely brought along enough oil for their lamps so they would be ready for the bridegroom even when he kept them waiting, and five of whom foolishly had not.

In its gospel context, following Jesus' prediction of the "end time" and the destruction of Jerusalem, it is an eschatological parable, a reflection of the early church's anxiety about the second coming of Christ (the bridegroom): he said he would be back. Where is he? So, in a semi-spontaneous "dialogue homily," Harold and John had gone back and forth about the "emotion of anticipation," about yearning for God to show himself—especially when we are in trouble—but also about our reluctance to actually let him break through, especially when he shows himself in ways we don't expect.

John: "You don't deny, Harold, that the twelve apostles had some advantages over us. They had not just Jesus' words but the force of his personality, the encouragement of his company, the warmth of his friendship."

Harold: "We don't know about that, John. Maybe Jesus didn't have a warm, encouraging personality. He had a quick temper and sometimes he lost it. After all, we know he cursed a fig tree for not having any figs when it wasn't even fig season. We do know that the apostles didn't really get loyal to Jesus until the

Resurrection—whatever that was—and we don't know how they would have responded to the crises the church faces today. Like AIDS for instance! What would the apostles tell a sexually active New York ghetto teenager? Practice chastity? Would they give out condoms or have them just take their chances with the old HIV? And where would the apostles be on celibacy and women priests? Since they were married, we have at least half the answer to that one."

Harold made John nervous during these pseudo-debates when every few weeks he dragged in by the back door the issues of celibacy and women's ordination. Theologically, John agreed with him; but somehow, he thought, although he had never said a word about it, there was something not right about Harold exercising his priesthood—as if he were faithful to the church's laws—when he was secretly married and, who knows, every night of the week he was sleeping with Trisha.

And what do you say about wise virgins to convicts?

"How long is this gonna take? Man, I'm freezin'." Rick Random didn't really want to be there either. But he was too polite, too passive to say no when John, cutting through Headly Lounge on the way out the door at 6:15 a.m., had spotted him curled up on the sofa, strumming his guitar, and invited him to come along and play for the prisoners while Susan sang.

Rick's long, thick, chestnut hair, which fell to his shoulders, was, like his rimless glasses, now flecked with big snowflakes; and he hunched forward, wrapping his arms and his blue ski jacket around his guitar case to keep it dry. His slender frame shivered—half because of cold, half because of fear.

"What am I gonna play? I don't know any hymns. And what if these guys are violent? What if they try a prison break or something?"

"Don't worry about it, Rick," Susan said, as she trotted ahead.

It was her third Sunday morning trip to the prison. There were things about Detweiler she didn't warm up to—his condescending humor, his pseudo-Prussian roleplaying—but to her there was something "Christian" about singing in a prison and she was forcing herself to go through with her project.

"Just improvise. Play anything you want that will set a good mood. If you can pick up some chords when I sing, that's great. If not, that's OK too. The point is, just try to act naturally. And don't worry. They won't hurt you." Susan did not know that, five years before, a cellblock had seized Father Detweiler and held him hostage for twenty-four hours until the warden negotiated his release, and that the previous rector had forbade him to invite students along on his prison mission.

The trio burst coughing and sneezing into the prison vestibule, brushing snow from their hats and coats and stamping it from their boots. Behind the reception counter a prison guard, an enormous, fat, black man, with a name tag that said "Gonzales," and wearing an unbuttoned blue uniform, slouched in a gray metal swivel chair, his eyes transfixed on the nine-inch TV screen three feet from his face.

His right jowl moved with a slow rhythm and he nestled a paper cup half filled with tobacco juice in his right hand. He was watching, expressionless, a Tom and Jerry cartoon. The cat, having discovered that it is the mouse's birthday, has buried dynamite sticks in a huge birthday cake, the wick of the dynamite disguised as a candle, and slid the cake, candle lit, outside the mouse's hole.

"Excuse me, officer. We would like passes for Cellblock D." John waited silently while Tom, impatient for Jerry to come out before the cake blows up, lifts the cake to examine the candle just as the dynamite explodes, and is propelled through the roof of the house in a red and black cloud of flame and smoke.

A barely perceptible smile curled the side of Gonzales' mouth, then his face sank back into sullen impassivity. "There's no church services in D this week," he said. "This week it's G."

"But Father Detweiler said it was D."

"I can't help that. I told you it's G. You can go up, but you gotta wait. They's servin' 'em breakfast."

Gonzales collected their driver's licenses and issued them plastic passes which they pinned to their shirts. A buzzer sounded and a metal door opened, then slammed behind them with a heavy clank. A green-painted elevator, its walls defaced with graffiti and still smelling of the wet, dirty mop that had sloshed through it the night before, hoisted them reluctantly to the third floor and opened its door to the corridor outside Cellblock G.

It was the women's wing.

John was not ready for this. He knew he was equally ignorant of both men's and women's prisons, but somehow he had forgotten that women were criminals and prisoners too, and he had merely presumed he would be preaching to men. Why were these women here? The men, he figured, would be drug dealers, car thieves and maybe murderers? Were these women prostitutes? What would he do with the homily? How would they take the parable about the ten wise and foolish virgins—or bridesmaids—all waiting for one bridegroom?

Rick and Susan pressed their faces up against the window of the gray metal door leading into the cellblock where the women—some in gray shapeless frocks, most in ugly sweat pants and sweat shirts, as if they were on their way to gym, rather than to a liturgy—lined up for the breakfast, a watery plop of oatmeal which the attendants ladled out to them from yellow thermos pots on a cart.

"Lookit that shit they hafta eat," said Rick. "It's worse'n what we get at school." He tugged affectionately at Susan's blond hair. They had barely met, but he was nervous and covered for it by acting playful.

"You've got a better vocabulary than that, Rick. Call it slop or swill." She smiled at him and rubbed her shoulder against his arm.

"It's not like *Women in Cages*," Rick added. "In the movies the women prisoners are all big and beautiful. They're white and half of them are blondes and they all have big breasts bursting out of their blouses. I don't think Hollywood knows about this place."

The cellblock was a big, long, sunless, fluorescent-lit, garage-like room, about the size of a small gymnasium, with two tiers of cells, with a narrow walkway in front of the cells, reaching up on three sides. In the center of the floor stood one lone metal table, like a picnic table, with benches attached on either side. About ten of the women huddled around the table, glum except for an occasional outburst, and ate their cereal from Styrofoam plates. The others, about forty of them, ate squatting on their haunches, leaning against the wall, or sitting on the stairs leading up to the cells. Nearly all were black.

Some, wrapped in khaki army blankets, slept curled up on the floor, as if they were homeless vagrants on the city streets, rather than prisoners in a city jail with a bunk in a cell they could call home. On either side of the open space, only partly concealed, was an open row of showers and toilets. Were they marched naked, Rick wondered, from their cells to the showers on designated days? Did they use the toilets in public under the gaze of fellow inmates and guards?

The guards gave the women about fifteen minutes to eat, then unlocked the door and let the visitors in. Susan took a broom from a closet near the toilets and started sweeping up Styrofoam cups, cigarettes, and paper napkins. John used his handkerchief to wipe up crumbs, ashes, spots of milk and spilled oatmeal on the metal table which was to become an altar. Although he felt awkward doing so, he took an alb, the long, white flowing vestment that completely covers the priest at mass, from his briefcase and pulled it on over his head. Then he placed about twenty hosts on a plate and poured a quarter of an inch of wine into his white ceramic chalice.

Rick, seated on the bench, removed his guitar from its case and began to strum it, hesitantly at first, then with some life, humming a wordless tune of his own he had devised in those aimless hours sitting on the edge of his bed in Headly Hall.

Half of the women retreated to their cells. The other half slowly circled the visitors—wary at first of the strangers, but now moving in like forest animals at night attracted to the warmth of a campfire.

Susan sang. She was a contralto and her voice had a deep, lush tone, and she looked directly at her stunned listeners not as if she were a performer on a stage and not as if she were a child trying to please adults, but rather like a fellow adult who is sharing some news, some simple truth.

> There is a balm in Gilead,
> To make the wounded whole,
> There is a balm in Gilead,
> To heal the sin-sick soul.
> Sometimes I feel discouraged and think
> My work's in vain,
> But then the Holy Spirit
> Revives my soul again.

John read the gospel loud enough for some of those who had gone back to their cells to hear it. Maybe they would get interested and come back. Then he spoke to the women for a few minutes.

"I know this gospel story in some ways may seem confusing to you and not make much sense. I guess the thing to remember is that in the first century, when this was written, in Jerusalem they had the custom of the bridal party—which is like the bridal party big weddings have today—escorting the groom to the bride's house in a big procession. But in this story, some of them didn't have enough oil to keep their lamps lit and so got left out of the party.

"So what does that have to do with us? Maybe we should say that the oil is like our ability to love. It's our responsibility to keep alive our power to love other people—no matter where we are. It's true to me back at the college and for you here. The power to love is something you can always give yourself. Even if someone takes away your freedom to go out in the street and to travel, no one can take away your freedom to forgive others, to think kind thoughts, to say nice things, to do favors for other people. So let's take a moment in prayer now and tell the Lord those things which we think we need."

After a few seconds of silence the prayers started to come.

"For my brutha."

"For my daughter."

"For me. It's my birthday." The speaker kept her eyes cast down—half afraid she would suddenly become the center of attention; half afraid she would not. She did not. Maybe, John thought, no one here knew her name.

"For my boyfriend Tyrone that he come and visits me."

"I want to thank the Lord that I am incarcerated at this time of my life, because if I wasn't incarcerated, I'd be dead."

John prayed for his deceased father and for his mother—whom he neglected by not writing and calling enough (though he didn't say that), and his sister, and his students and—with his upcoming tenure decision in mind—for his "future," whatever the Lord wanted that future to be.

He offered up the bread and wine and continued into the eucharistic prayer. In imitation of Jesus at the Last Supper he took the large host in his fingertips and lifted it up for all to see.

> The night before he died
> Jesus took bread
> blessed and broke it
> and gave it to his disciples with the words,
> Take this all of you and eat it,
> for this is my body
> which will be given up for you.

But the last words were drowned out by a roaring Niagara, a choking, coughing, echoing rush of water. An inmate had flushed a toilet, and the noise reverberated from the screaming swirl in the bowl, up the tile walls of the open bathroom, magnified by the cellblock's sacred silence.

They said the Lord's Prayer together. Or tried to say it. "Give us this day" . . . the doors at the far end of the room swung open with a clang, and three guards burst into the cellblock, then into the third cell from the door. John could see two bare, black legs kicking in an upper bunk, and a voice louder than any he had heard in his life screamed, "Get your hands off me, you motherfuckers!"

He tried to act as if nothing had happened, as if the solemnity of Christ's sacrifice had not been shattered by the most obscene expression mankind had devised. He moved through the women and greeted each one with a touch and a smile at the Peace. He looked for the one who had declared her birthday, but now, in their gray sweat suits and black faces, they were once again all alike.

At communion, although he suspected that very few of them were Catholics, he invited them all to come forward and receive. As each approached him with either an outstretched palm or an open mouth, tongue extended to receive the wafer, he was disconcerted, even shaken, by how forlorn, pathetic, sometimes ugly each one seemed. Did the jailers conspire to keep them ugly, to squelch whatever loveliness every woman has if she can but love herself enough to care for her appearance? Scars and bumps and sores blighted their faces and hands.

Again and again their spittle stuck to his fingers as he placed the sacred host on their tongues. He had read the stories of Damian the Leper, Saint Peter Claver, and Dorothy Day who had forced themselves to kiss the puss-oozing wounds of prisoners and slaves in order to overcome their revulsion, to demonstrate the radical commitment implicit in Christ's love. But nothing could induce him to kiss the lips before him this morning. Could he possibly pick up a disease? What if he were to unconsciously touch his own face, his mouth right afterward? What if one with sores in her mouth were to drop the host after he had put it on her tongue? He would have to pick it up off the floor and, with her spit on it, consume it himself, wouldn't he? Could he get AIDS? He was ashamed for even entertaining these thoughts. He was supposed to love these women, and he told himself he did. He did.

Susan sang and Rick played and began to sing too. He had a light tenor voice and he could harmonize.

> What a Friend we have in Jesus
> All our sins and griefs to bear!
> What a privilege to carry
> Everything to God in prayer!

John gave the last blessing. A few of the women, reluctant to look them in the eyes, thanked them. One grabbed his sleeve.

"Father, can you help me?"

"I don't know. What can I do?"

"Can you get a message to my son?"

"I . . . I'll try. You'll have to give me his address."

"Oh, he right here. He downstairs in Cellblock B. You just tell him his momma . . . she upstairs in G."

"I'll see what I can do."

The others withdrew to their cells or huddled around the TV set in the corner. Then John and Rick and Susan went back out into the snow. John reminded himself to wash his hands when he got home.

Louise McKinney

Wedding Party

Tonight the night
enters big-sky country,
Summer heat seeps into purple
stretching from horizon to horizon,
fifty stars hang like tin badges,
and chinooks sweep the night places
left to them:
cornfields, barns or paved car lots.

Inside the hall dinner is done.
Faces down the red flocked wall
bud in loamy dark and germ of conversation.
Others watching others just smile.

The Elks Club swells,
pink hearts spell out "Husband & Wife"
in sequined words.
A country duo harmonize
on love and wrongdoing
as if it were that simple.

The elk on the wall
with wan bead-eyes and dusty horns
weathers these storms of celebration.

But at midnight everything sings!
Dresses whirl. The bridesmaids' gowns
make hurricanes of pink silk sideways,
drunks prop the bar,
children run counterclockwise,
zippers, ties and buttons
are finally undone

and a drunken bride turns, shoeless,
in one corner of the room.

Waterfall

Just west of Pincher Creek you put on your gloves.
I lean to the windshield,
press my breath and palms to frost formed there.
But the holes fill with light as I make them
and we are blind again.

Our truck holds on the edge of foothills,
leans on great lummoxing turns;
I work my brake like an Easterner, primed with history
and new events,
expecting frontier, I get it.

Peak-high we climb over cities of firs,
hatch and cross-hatch, settled on each ridge.
Elk gaze from outcrop, their racks
click-click
in the strange thickening
found at this height.

In Red Rock, we leave the bells of skiers
fastened to the air behind us, and on foot now
hike higher, cutting our lungs on the cold,
to where a waterfall knuckles past—
and is too close for good pictures.

Eye

Eye is stone, a mark on the map of the face
Of a whole province in ruin
A small hill eroded by rain
Eye is water
Eye is wood
Eye is damproot-tangled
Under leaves that shiver and turn

Eye is center of the arc of the sky
Hole where stars can pour through

And eye is a fossil unfound
The print that remains (barely there) and remains
Eye written, eye is historian
Eye is spectator

Eye a drawn shade filtering light
Or eye, wide-open, a stark white room
With windows
By which to sit and stare, sometimes into nothing
But the artist's eye is still-life detail
Gold chalice, crude cup
Eye as line, light, color—content
All he receives, yet still
Not enough

Eye is just this
A capacity (sees what it will see)
Wide skies, a lake,
Leaf God-given green
A green leaf
With light shining through!

Hand

At our fingertips, blood
stops briefly and turns
around again
doubling on itself
and gaining energy
in such small space.
Tributaries, where textures
leave liquid impressions
(for memory)
eddy in dark corners,
head out again.
Blood is this constant,
dark-red, looping.

Hand, a landscape close up
dunes swept down over
bones, over the knuckles,
making shadowed hillocks.
But even closer skin is rock,
scored deeply,
hatched with fissures and veins
showing stress where it
bears up after all,
craggy as a cliff.

Eventually the hand becomes
the fossil it is,
horn called nails
falls out.
And what's left may tell our age,
perhaps a name—
that solitary sign
who we were.

Blues Fragment

For Avery

He say:
"Baby,

Life take you *out* there
And bring you back in."

She say:
"Life make you wonder
If you gonna live again."

Louise's Kitchen

Dark as earth
from the riverbed,
her mud pies steamed
with spring rains
instead of hot berries and figs.
Topped not with cream,
but trimmed with reeds,
green grasses, twigs.
No one ate her soft salad leaves
of pussy willow buds
and wings of bees,
all springtime-sprinkled,
tossed on a breeze.

Steppingstone-leap,
and rubber boots roam,
child in the forest,
Mother at home.

Butter dripped
from a buttercup chin,
dents de lion
stained the hand,
to blow its seeds
a honeyed breath
sweet with lilac
and clover meads.

Pine needles
swept up on knees
made the forest floor
a bed of ease
for a weary child: Louise.

Steppingstone-leap
and rubber boots roam,
girl in the forest,
Mother at home.

The Heron and the Deer

I with my companion walked
At dusk, following the shore.
So little need was there to talk,
I answered her no more.

I answered her no more
And the ocean echoed calm.
Over tide pools we would pore
Where starfish drift along.

Where seas stars drift along
There we spied him perched on high,
His bill scissor-like and strong,
Blue on gray at eventide.

Blue on gray at eventide
The great heron heard our step,
Staring out one yellow eye,
yet to the rock he kept.

To the rock he kept
When the sudden trampling came,
And out a bush it leapt!
A mule deer that was lame.

A deer the hunter lamed
Bolted straight into the sea,
And in wild astonished pain
Swam round in front of me.

Swam round in front of me.

Merlin

A cat named Merlin once I met.
His chin was tufted gray.
His only purpose was to get
The jays to stay away.

He sat and stared, stared he and sat,
With even whiskers still,
As raucous jays swooped at the cat
Poised on the windowsill.

Or, balanced on the balcony,
Ten scimitars unsheathed,
With mysteries of cat wizardry
And silence of a thief.

So when you heard a fracas shrill
In leaves of trees up high,
T'was Merlin—closed in for the kill
Jays dark against the sky.

For Merlin had a wandlike tail,
A glossy cloak of stripes,
His topaz eyes made flesh turn pale,
Cut keenly as a knife.

And as far as I can tell you,
As far as I can see,
that yellow gaze drew noisy blue
From branches of the trees.

Was it spell or incantation?
Or tooth as sharp as claw?
Was it prestidigitation—
a lightning sleight of paw?

I think that I can safely say,
Whenever *he* was near,
The jays knew best to stay away:
To fly. Or disappear!

Have You Been to Mississippi?

For Lowell Gasparini

Have you been to Mississippi,
Where the clouds are warm and whippy,
And ice cream cold and drippy,
Where the waves are wet?

The Films of Theo Angelopoulos: Beyond The Borders

Andrew Horton

Note: *Excerpted with the author's permission from the original essay.*

How many borders do we have to cross to get home?
from **The Suspended Step of The Stork**

The world needs cinema now more than ever. It may be the last important form of resistance to the deteriorating world in which we live. In dealing with borders, boundaries, the mixing of languages and cultures today, I am trying to seek a new humanism, new way.
—**Theo Angelopoulos**

Refuse the life of anarchy;
Refuse the life devoted to one master.
The Chorus, Aeschylus' ***Eumenides***

It is a cool September evening in 1975 in Thessaloniki, Greece's second largest city. A noisy standing room only crowd is packed into the major cinema, the site of the annual Greek Film Festival. The lights dim and director Theo Angelopoulos' third feature film, *O Thiasos (The Traveling Players)* begins. It is a three hour and forty minute epic about Greece from 1939, through World War II and the subsequent Civil War up to the beginning of 1952. But there is more. The film has no main character, is shot almost entirely in long shots which are also long takes, often lasting several minutes. Add to this that most of the film is shot with the pale light and colors of dawn or dusk in Northern Greece particularly during winter and you begin to realize in content and form, this is a work as unlike the dominant form of cinema in the world—Hollywood—as could be imagined.

Would more than a handful of true cineastes respond to such a demanding project? Several hours later the answer was clear from the standing ovation.

That evening was memorable for all present including myself. *The Traveling Players* became an immediate sensation. In less than a year it went on to be the largest selling Greek film ever, to win numerous international awards, and eventually to be voted by The Italian Film Critics Association as the most important film in the world for the decade of the 1970's as well as one of the Top Films of the History of Cinema by the International Film Critics Association.

Seven features have followed for a total of ten: *Reconstruction* (1970), *The Hunters* (1977), *Megalexandros* (1980), *Voyage to Cythera* (1984), *The Beekeeper* (1986), *Landscape in The Mist* (1988), *The Suspended Step of The Stork* (1991), and *Ulysses' Gaze* (1995). Six of these, furthermore, belong to trilogies that Angelopoulos himself has acknowledged. His "historical" trilogy: *Day of '36, The Traveling Players,* and *Megalexandros* cover Greek history from the turn of the century through 1952, with an "epilogue" film being *The Hunters* which jumps to the present (the 1970's) to suggest how the past has haunted contemporary Greece. And Angelopoulos has dubbed *Voyage to Cythera, The Beekeeper,* and *Landscape in The Mist* as his trilogy of "silence."

What effect has this filmmaker from Greece had on others? *The New York Times* wrote of *Landscape in The Mist,* "There are sights in the film that once seen cannot be forgotten." (Holden) Raymond Durgnat states, "Angelopoulos' long takes approach, in their despair, their counterparts in Tarkovsky." Another critic writes that, "Angelopoulos' shattering power resists conventional naming," while Michael Wilmington calls Angelopoulos "one of the cinema's great unsolved mysteries": a filmmaker working far from Hollywood in every sense who suddenly bursts "upon us full force."

Few filmmakers have ever shared such honors and touched such nerves within their home cultures. What Angelopoulos succeeded in accomplishing in 1975, before, and since, is our concern. More specifically, I wish to explore his cinema in the context of his Greek heritage including history, myth, literature, folk culture, music, and cinema. And I am interested in the wider context of Angelopoulos' resistance to Hollywood narrative and subsequent relationship to world cinema.

Theo Angelopoulos is a serious maker of films ("uncompromising" is the adjective often assigned to him by critics and audiences alike). This is to say that while he is deeply concerned with the aesthetics of his work, he is, ultimately, using/working in cinema with "other" intentions as the above quotation suggests.

I remember being asked in Moscow in 1988 by eager "kino club" viewers, who I thought the *spiritual* leader of American cinema was at the moment. Spielberg, Scorcese, Woody Allen, Spike Lee? Of course they had an answer for Soviet cinema: Andrei Tarkovsky. It was no use trying to explain that nobody in Los Angeles or Culver City would understand the question, let alone try to answer it.

But the question does originate from a very different concept of what "serious" cinema offers an audience. And within that framework, Angelopoulos has served as, if not a "spiritual leader," at least as an outspoken artist who has looked deeply into Greek culture and come up with his films which follow Plato's dictum quoted in the beginning of Angelopoulos' latest film, *Ulysses' Gaze,* "To know a soul, a soul must look into a soul." What that looking has brought forth from Angelopoulos and those who appreciate him is a vision of the *other* Greece, the one that has been neglected, repressed, rejected, covered up. It is a Greece of rural spaces, long silences, mythic echoes, missed connections, winter landscapes, wanderers, refugees and actors without a stage or audience. This is not the Greece on travel posters, of the Parthenon, or of a small country trying to hold its own in an emerging United European community. The Greece in Angelopoulos' films is clearly "somewhere else" than Athens and the other urban areas and the centers of tourism. And by extension, this *other Greece* is the *other life* that each of us would rather sweep under the rug, put under lock and key, turn our backs on.

In Greece there is definitely a dedicated following for Angelopoulos' work. But it should be added that as Greece's best known and most critically acclaimed director abroad, Angelopoulos has, in contrast, often had to face indifference and opposition at home. Some Greeks interviewed, for instance, who greatly appreciated *The Traveling Players,* have accused Angelopoulos of being too uncompromising in exposing the darker corners of the

Greek experience. Others admire his talent but on a very practical level say, "When you've worked hard all day, and you want to go to the cinema in the evening, it's hard to get into the frame of mind necessary to 'enjoy' the length and intensity of an Angelopoulos film."

Angelopoulos smiles when asked about such reactions. "I am in a very strange position in Greece," he comments. "I have fanatic enemies and fanatic followers. That's all that I can say!"

History is not dead: it is only taking a nap.

—**Theo Angelopoulos**

The best of them (writers/artists) are realistic, and paint life as it is, but because every line is permeated, as with sap, by the consciousness of a purpose, you are aware not only of life as it is, but of life as it ought to be, and that captivates you.

—**Anton Chekhov**

Two shots. First: A desolate village appears on the screen in black and white as an unidentified narrator explains that this village in Northern Epirus, near Albania, had a population of 1,250 in 1939 and 85 in 1965. Second: What appears to be a jerky black and white silent film from the turn of the century: on the screen we see an actor playing Odysseus, climbing out of the sea, washed up on the shore at long last of Ithaca. He pauses and looks out at the camera and thus at us, "living at the end of the 20th century."

Theo Angelopoulos of Greece has emerged as one of the most original voices in world cinema in a remarkable series of ten feature films made since 1970.

That he remains virtually unknown in the United States despite his Academy Award nominations and a major retrospective at the Museum of Modern Art in New York in 1992, simply adds to the need for a study which attempts to account for the enduring importance of his work. For his is both a contemporary voice within Greek culture and a filmmaker within the context of world cinema sharing influences and affinities as divergent as those of Jean Renoir, Ozu, Tarkovsky, Jansco, Antonioni and the Hollywood musical.

The two shots mentioned embrace his first feature, *Reconstruction* (1970) and his latest, *Ulysses' Gaze* (1994). But more important, they point to the twin dimension of Angelopoulos' vision which both "documents" (thus the documentary look and statistical sound track to the opening shot) and fictionalizes, building on/alluding to a Greek past (Odysseus as captured in a silent film at the beginning of the century).

That history and myth cross in complicated and provocative ways in Angelopoulos' films is clear from the context of the silent Odysseus shot. The film is being screened in a bombed out cinema in Sarajevo in 1994 while bombs burst around the building. And the person viewing the film is a Greek film director who has searched throughout the Balkans for this "missing" film he has been told was the first made in the Balkans. In a single shot, contemporary horror—the Bosnian war, individual destiny, myth (Odysseus), and the history of cinema (the first Balkan film) come together.

What does the image mean or suggest?

It is one of Angelopoulos' traits and, we might add, virtues, that he does not "explain" or preach. The image is simply there, intriguing in its own right, open to multiple readings and evoking a number of emotions. But clearly the filmmaker has orchestrated form and content to *invite* us or even *compel* us to go beyond the image itself and establish "meaning." As Nikos Kolovos has noted in his book-length study of these films, Angelopoulos believes in treating each image with "lucidite": like a poet, selecting his images carefully, but letting the image speak for itself. Angelopoulos stands apart even within his own culture. We search in vain for the straight forward strong drama, comedy, and tragedy found in Jules Dassin's *Never on Sunday* (1960) or Michael Cacoyannis' *A Girl in Black* (1957), *Zorba the Greek* (1962), or *Iphigenia* (1978), or the riveting pace and simple dogmatism of a film such as Costa-Gavras' *Z* (1969). There is none of the bright blue cinematography and romantic stereotyping of Greece found in films such as *Mediterraneo* and *Shirley Valentine* in which Greece serves as a pastoral ideal landscape for foreigners to discover true sexual liberation and personal happiness dancing by the sea.

Journal: Saturday, October 20th

Richard Grayson

---

9 p.m.

Because of my first Saturday class at BCC-South, I didn't get to the trial till 12:30 p.m., and they wouldn't let me in during the defense's closing arguments. However, after a break, I got to hear Pedro's final talk to the jury and the judge's charge, which I told Rogow when I saw him in the men's room should be called "Miller time" for Miller v. California.

I figured I had time to get a salad at Wendy's on SE 17th Street, and when I got back, I sat down in the courtroom next to one of the alternate jurors, who told all the reporters he never considered a guilty verdict. I'd have been shocked at one myself after I'd heard one of the prosecutors, Pedro, say, in an elevator with only the two of us in it (I think he was mostly talking to himself), "This case was the worst piece of crap I've ever had." I realized I'd viewed Pedro and Leslie as the enemy, but they were only underpaid civil servants doing their jobs.

Despite the anticipation of a favorable verdict, I also remembered how stunned I was at the Freeman guilty verdict. (And at that time the alternate juror said she would have voted for acquittal, too.) I talked a lot to Jeanne DeQuince, who'd been writing for *USA Today*, and

Susan Grey from WINZ and Charlie Freeman and others. When the buzzer sounded at 4:10 p.m., everyone rushed around as word came in that the jury had reached a verdict. The courtroom filled up with media people and spectators, and the TV camera was moved to the witness stand so that it could get the defense table's reaction to the verdict. When the court clerk read the first verdict, finding Luke not guilty, he jumped for joy and the courtroom erupted into cheers. I've seen the scene on videotape—it led the *NBC Nightly News* as well as the local shows—and through a trick of perspective I appear to be sitting immediately behind Luke Campbell and in front of Charlie Freeman. Chills ran down my arms, and my eyes started welling up with tears. I didn't shout, but I felt good, and in some way this verdict made up for what happened in the Freeman case—but not quite.

It was an exciting scene as flashbulbs popped and the lights from videocams glared, and a press conference was set up in the adjoining courtroom. Rogow spoke first, about the freedom of speech, even offensive speech, and the other lawyers said their bit, but of course Luke Campbell was the star, and he handled himself well. We had a fair jury, he told the crowd, and he made some nice remarks about the supportive people of Broward County. I know it's a victory for the First Amendment, but there's still the federal appeal on Judge Gonzalez's ruling, and Freeman's appeal, and next week's trial as well. How many other obscenity cases will be brought against artists and performers?

Today in my own ENC 1102 class, I had an experience which tells me that censorship forces are more alive than ever. Actually, the class seems like a delightful group: all adults, some professional people, even some who say they enjoy writing and literature. But when we came back after our break, I did what I'd done before in

1102, read aloud one of my favorite stories, Flannery O'Connor's "A Good Man Is Hard to Find."

Unfortunately, we never got around to discussing the story because one woman immediately raised her hand and demanded to know why "a book like this" was allowed to be published, much less used in a school. The word "nigger," used twice in dialogue of the grandmother, so blinded her that she couldn't—despite all my reasonable talk and the patient arguments of the class—see that it wasn't the author of the story insulting *her* personally.

It really made me feel lousy, even though the woman made it clear she wasn't accusing *me* of racism. Not being able to explain the difference between a person's racial insult and attributing a racist remark to an unsympathetic and foolish character in a story over forty years old—that just about made me want to give up teaching altogether.

If we can't represent life as it is or what it was, then can artists do *anything*? Is there any difference between this woman wanting to censor the text and Broward County trying to censor 2 Live Crew? What advice would Prof. Henry Louis Gates give me if I wrote him? Probably I can manage to get an op-ed piece out of this, but I'd rather have avoided having the experience. I haven't read today's or yesterday's *Times,* and I'm too tired to do anything but close my eyes.

— It's still Saturday, 10 p.m., and I can't stop my mind from racing. That incident in class today bothers me tremendously. Do I need to be accused, even indirectly, of racism because I teach—and enjoy—a story that twice contains the word "nigger"? Is what happened to Salman Rushdie going to happen to every writer who offends a particular group? Are fewer people intelligent enough, as I am, to appreciate writers and artists who nevertheless are racist, sexist, anti-Semitic, homophobic? I like Henry Adams and Céline and numerous writers who were notorious Jew-haters.

When I was in grade school, we talked about the ideal of "tolerance"—that condescending word. Is the new tolerance lack of tolerance? OK, we're dealing with BCC 1102 students here; these are the same people who last year thought the deliberately awful stories in Crad Kilodney's *Worst Canadian Stories* anthologies were artfully written.

Maybe this is just another one of a thousand signals blaring, telling me to stop teaching college English. I'm sick of other people, and I feel anger toward the woman who took all the joy out of today for me. When I should be ecstatic over the 2 Live Crew verdict, I can't relax because I see threats to free expression popping up everywhere now. Instead of feeling relieved and hopeful, I just want to get away from my fellow human beings. And do I need to worry about this when I'm going bankrupt? Last night I dreamed I was driving all around Staten Island, and now I want to get back to that place I created in my mind and never come out.

Biographies

Richard Grayson, a Brooklyn, New York, native, was born in 1951. Since 1975, more than 150 of his short stories have appeared in *Texas Quarterly, California Quarterly, Florida Review, Transatlantic Review, Epoch,* and *Shenandoah.* Grayson's books of short stories include *With Hitler in New York* (Taplinger, 1979), *Lincoln's Doctor's Dog* (White Ewe, 1982), *I Brake for Delmore Schwartz* (Zephyr, 1983), and *Narcissism and Me* (Mule & Mule, 1989). He is also a journalist, with articles and columns appearing in *People Magazine, The Miami Herald,* and *New York Newsday* among other publications.

Recipient of numerous fellowships and scholarships, Grayson holds an MA and MFA from City University of New York, graduated with high honors from the University of Florida's College of Law, and recently accepted a post as visiting assistant in law at that school's Center for Government Responsibility, in Gainesville.

Andrew S. Horton resides in New Orleans, Louisiana, where he teaches film and literature at Loyola University and is director of the New Orleans Film Festival. A graduate of the University of Illinois, where he received a PhD in comparative literature and cinema studies, Horton has journeyed extensively in Eastern Europe and Russia. His travels to those countries have resulted in a variety of educational exchanges, and in Horton's creation of the first International Conference on Soviet Film, which in its founding year was attended by a select group of twenty film scholars from the United States, the Soviet Union and Canada. Horton coordinated a second Loyola University/Moscow Mass Culture

Conference, held in the Russian Republic during the summer of 1992.

Horton's publications include, among others, *The Zero Hour: Glasnost and Soviet Cinema in Translation* (Princeton University Press), *Laughter With a Lash: Inside Soviet Film Satire* (Cambridge University Press), *Writing the Character-Centered Script* (University of California Press) and *Play It Again Sam: Re-takes on Remakes* (University of Texas Press).

Lisa Kahn, native of Berlin, is a professor of German and resides in Houston and Round Top, Texas. She is one of the editors at *Trans-Lit*, a bi-annual literary magazine published by the Society for Contemporary American Literature in German. She has published three anthologies, a prose volume and ten volumes of poetry. Mellen Poetry Press has published the English version of her poems on Crete, *KPHTH, Fertile and Full of Grace* (1992), and her most recent German work, *Atlantische Brucke* (1992). She received the Cross of Merit of the Federal Republic of Germany in 1990 and the 1993 Pegasus Award of the Austin-based Poetry in the Arts Association.

Steven G. Kellman is professor of comparative literature at The University of Texas at San Antonio and film critic for *The Texas Observer.* His recent books include *The Plague: Fiction and Resistance* and, as editor, *Perspectives on Raging Bull.*

Margin of Hydra lives incognito on Earth, engaged as a professional globetrotter, novelist, and safari bush guide. A descendant of clipper ship captains, offspring of a spaceship designer, Margin was raised in the tradition of the Adventurous Voyage. From Aurora Borealis to the Southern Cross, Margin has seen the Earth and has intimate knowledge of its strangest quirks and natives. Margin's book, *Travels with Ninotchka* received the Hydra Voyagers Award for Best Earth Journal. Margin is currently on global safari, training novice explorers in the art and science of Earth Travel. A member of PEN Hydra, Margin is the first alien novelist to appear in *Southern Lights*.

Skye Kathleen Moody: Writer, photographer and former East African bush guide, Skye Kathleen Moody has written about social and environmental conditions in Asia, East Africa and Eastern Europe, and about environmental issues in Northern Europe. Under the name Kathy Kahn, she wrote *Hillbilly Women*, an award-winning book about life in Southern Appalachia. Her book, *Fruits of our Labor*, about Soviet and American life, was published under the same name. She has written two one-act plays, one produced at the 92nd Street Y in New York, the other in Seattle.

Moody's photographs have been exhibited throughout the world, most recently in Sichuan Province, China. A native of the Pacific Northwest, she lives in New Orleans.

Robert Phillips' poems are "better than literary—they are literature," says Robert B. Shaw in *Poetry*. Author of five full-length volumes of verse and two works of fiction, a noted scholar with four books of criticism to his credit and reviews appearing in such esteemed journals as *The Paris Review*, *The New Yorker*, *Chicago Review* and *The New Republic*, Phillips is one of the outstanding American writers of his generation. His newest collection of poetry, *Breakdown Lane* (The Johns Hopkins University Press, 1994), gathers recollections of a childhood spent on Delaware's eastern shore, elegies for the recent dead in American arts, extended metaphors on suburban existence and a section of poems in which the poet courts, wins, then loses the Muse.

Currently, Phillips is a professor of English at the University of Houston where he is the director of that school's creative writing program. He has been poetry reviewer for *The Houston Post* from 1992 to the present, and acts as literary executor for the estate of Delmore Schwartz.

Raymond A. Schroth, S.J.: Born in Trenton, New Jersey, Schroth has spent his life as a Jesuit, a journalist, and teacher. After graduating from Fordham University—where he majored in American Civilization and was an editor for the *Fordham Ram*—in 1955, he served as an anti-aircraft artillery officer in Germany for two years and joined the Society of Jesus in 1957. Ordained a priest in 1967, he obtained his PhD in American Thought and Culture at The George Washington University and taught journalism at Fordham until 1979. During that time he also served as associate editor and book editor of *Commonweal* magazine.

Currently, Schroth teaches journalism at Loyola University in New Orleans, Louisiana. He has published three books: *The Eagle and Brooklyn: A Community Newspaper* (Greenwood); *Books for Believers: 35 Books Every Catholic Should Read* (Paulist); and, with Jeff Theilman, *Volunteer: With the Poor in Peru* (Paulist). In recent summers he has traveled to Gabon, South Africa, Peru, and Iraq to educate himself, write articles, and take pictures. His articles and reviews on politics, religion, and literature have appeared in *Commonweal, America, The National Catholic Reporter, The Los Angeles Times,* and *New York Newsday* among other publications. Raymond Schroth's new book, *The American Journey of Eric Sevareid,* will be published by Steerforth Press this spring.

Marian Schwartz studied Russian literature at Harvard University, Leningrad State University, and the University of Texas at Austin. In 1976, she moved to New York City, where she worked as an in-house editor for two years. By 1978, she had already published translations of several short stories and *Landmarks*, a collection of philosophical essays that had a seminal influence on the prerevolutionary Russian intelligentsia.

In 1981, Schwartz was asked to co-translate *Woman of Iron*, by Nina Berberova, with whom she was closely associated until her death in 1993. In 1985, her translation of Berberova's "Sentence Commuted" was the first-place winner in *The Literary Review*'s Novella-in-Translation contest.

In the past five years, Schwartz has published five books of translation—fiction and nonfiction—and numerous stories by a variety of authors. Her translation of Edvard Radzinsky's *The Last Tsar: The Life and Death of Nicholas II* was on the *New York Times* bestseller list for twelve weeks and has since appeared in paperback and on audiocassette. Her most recent publication is the translation of Vassily Peskov's *Lost in the Taiga: One Russian Family's Fifty-Year Struggle for*

Survival and Religious Freedom in the Siberian Wilderness. Marian Schwartz lives and translates in Austin, Texas.

June Akers Seese: Author of numerous short stories and of three novels published by the internationally prestigious Dalkey Archive Press, Seese has emerged as a vivid, prolific voice on the current literary scene. In *What Waiting Really Means* (1990), she made her debut as a novelist, and followed up with *Is This What Other Women Feel Too?* (1991) Seese's third book, *James Mason and the Walk-in Closet and Collected Stories*, gathers some of the writer's best short fiction. Readers may be familiar with Seese's stories published in such journals as *Catalyst, Carolina Quarterly, Lullwater Review, Witness,* and *South Carolina Review*.

Formerly a native of Detroit, Michigan, and graduate in English at Wayne State University, Seese taught secondary school for eight years. Now a resident of Atlanta, Georgia, with her husband and two sons, she has been an instructor in creative writing for Spelman College, an editor, a teacher of literature at the Callanwolde Fine Arts Center and producer of Uptown/On the Town, the city's long-running literary performance series.

In recent years, Seese has given numerous lectures and readings. Her plays have been performed for the Theatrical Outfit and at the Branson Theatre of Duke University.

Sergei Task is a fiction writer, playwright, and translator. A graduate of Moscow State University, he is currently pursuing an MFA in theater at the University of Iowa.

Guest Editor and Contributor
Louise McKinney: Originally from Toronto, Canada, Louise McKinney's poems have appeared in various North American literary journals, including *Poetry Canada Review, Toronto Life, Grain* and *Wind.* She is presently at work completing a book of children's verse, and placing her first poetry manuscript, entitled *Landfall.*

For more than a decade, McKinney has earned her living as a freelance writer/editor in both magazine and book publishing. Her articles, reviews and essays have appeared in *The World and I, Canadian Literature, Maclean's, The Globe & Mail, Toronto Life* and *Destinations,* among other publications. She was poetry editor for *Toronto Life* magazine from 1986 to 1990, where she helped produce a special fund-raising literary supplement in conjunction with PEN International. McKinney continues her work with PEN as a "Friend of PEN" and as guest editor of *Southern Lights.* She lives with her husband in New Orleans, Louisiana. They are expecting their first child.

About *PEN*

PEN American Center, a non-profit incorporation, is an affiliate of International PEN: an association of writers—poets, playwrights, essayists, editors, novelists—with centers in Europe, Asia, Africa, Australia and the Americas.

An international society of poets, essayists and novelists (thus, the PEN acronym), PEN was founded in 1921 in London, as a society for authors and translators of literary works, with the primary focus of promoting collegiality among its members and freedom of expression throughout the world. Later, PEN added editors of literature to its membership. Today, International PEN has approximately 10,000 members, and, of those, 2,800 are members of PEN America. PEN American Center/South (formerly "PEN Gulf South") represents seven states of PEN members: Texas, Arkansas, Georgia, Louisiana, Mississippi, Alabama and Florida. From this small but rich source of American literature, *Southern Lights* has distilled this first annual volume of contemporary works.